FATHERING
THE NEXT
GENERATION

FATHERING THE NEXT GENERATION

MEN MENTORING MEN

William J. Jarema

CROSSROAD • NEW YORK

1994

The Crossroad Publishing Company
370 Lexington Avenue, New York, NY 10017

Copyright © 1994 by William J. Jarema

Printed in the United States of America

Library of Congress Cataloging-in-Publication Data

Jarema, William J.
    Fathering the next generation : men mentoring men / William J.
Jarema.
       p. cm.
    Includes bibliographical references.
    ISBN 0-8245-1442-4
    1. Fathers and sons. 2. Fatherhood—Religious aspects.
3. Parenting—Religious aspects. 4. Fathers—Psychology.
I. Title
HQ755.85.J37 1995
306.874'2—dc20
                                          94-33955
                                            CIP

To the men who dared to talk about
their need and longing for a father,
men whose courage allowed them to share
their family secrets and personal wounds,
thereby mentoring the next generation of men
who will become fathers for others.

Contents

Part Two
THE EMPOWERED MALE AS FATHER
Five Healthy Fathering Styles

Part Three
WHERE DO I BEGIN?

Preface

I have had the opportunity to interview more than a thousand men throughout the United States. Together we have shared sacred time and space as we remembered our fathers. The willingness of these men to confess their own inadequacies as fathers has provided invaluable insight.

This book is a collection of ideas, examples, and true stories, related to me at these various gatherings. It is not a recipe book for male parenting or fathering; it is not my purpose to underestimate the subtle differences in styles of fathering. I do hope to provide deeper insight into a request I have received from many of the men with whom I have worked: "How can I become a better father? Give me some practical male parenting and fathering behaviors that will enable me to break negative patterns and become a good father."

As you read through this book, some of these stories will corroborate your own personal experiences. If you hurt and grieve as you revisit painful moments and memories, share this with someone. Don't keep your memories to yourself. Don't keep the pain inside. Don't give into the lie that it doesn't hurt or embarrass you. Don't reduce how you feel.

If you can't find someone with whom to share, then call the Mercy Center at 1-800-MERCY04. If I am not available, one of my staff will be there to talk with you, to listen to your story and be with you in the remembering. We will help you find a men's group or other support services. We will encourage you to move deeper into your personal ownership of self as father, man, son.

Thanks to Henry Smith, who over the years has been my rock and earth. Without his friendship I'm not sure I would have made it to this point in my life and career.

There would have been no beginning of this book unless I was encouraged and kicked in the pants by Tim Fogle. He provided me with a computer, desk, and room in his home and the booster shot needed to begin this adventure.

Thanks to the staff of the Mercy Center for Healing the Whole Person, Colorado Springs, Colorado: Mary Howard, Kim Mersman, Margaret Hensen, Elizabeth Wippern. And thanks to the satellite programs that gave me places to meet with men from around the United States.

Thanks to my Aunt Carol Bearss for her patience and willingness to sort through these many pages and help to make them readable. Thanks to Lee Ballantyne, Midge Cossentino, Kathy Frankmore, John Merrit, Harry Tanner, Kathleen Rapp, Adrienne LaMantia, Debbie Lowery, Mary Ann Wojtaszek, Ron Asselin, Cullen Wheelock, Marilyn Jarema, Kelly Snover, and Roger Kittridge.

Thanks to my editor, Lynn Schmitt. Her encouragement and belief in me helped me to complete this manuscript.

Fathers and Sons

——————— ✑ ———————

I remember the day clearly—September 8, 1988. Jake sat in my office with a look of terror and anguish. His voice was shaky and raspy from crying, and his face was flushed with embarrassment. He leaned far forward in his chair as though he were about to fall on the floor. Looking right at me, he pleaded, "Help me! I'm becoming my father." After a time of wailing and moaning, Jake grew quiet enough for me to ask him, "What exactly do you mean, you're becoming your father?"

In the next hour I came to understand Jake's fear and bewilderment. Like many stories of men I had heard in therapy, his story revealed that in spite of all his efforts to the contrary his worst fears were coming true.

Jake repeated his inner vow with rage and anger: "I'll never be like my old man! I'll never treat my kids the way he treated me and my brothers and sisters. Every time my dad had a bad day, I suffered for it. He was a selfish, angry son-of-a-bitch!" What followed was a thorough character assassination and detailed inventory of faults, failings, and sins of his dad:

* *When my dad came home angry, he would look to find some fault in my house chores. Then he would begin the nagging, the name-calling, and, finally, the beating. He would usually end up throwing me against the dining room wall. If I got up, he would do it again and again until I couldn't get up or until my mother would step in between us and beg him to stop.*

11

On the sidelines were my siblings standing there in horror and terror. They were afraid to say or do anything. And if they did, they would have to pay the price of verbal or physical abuse.

The problem grew with intensity the older and bigger I got. But then it took longer to keep me down on that floor. One day when I was sixteen years old, the "big one" occurred. I had been involved in football and other sports that, I can see now, prepared me for what I was about to do. My dad came home with that look. He was hunting for a subject on which to begin his routine of torture and rage. He began to pick on my younger brother, Dave. Slowly he baited Dave to reveal enough evidence to convict him of some minor error in his house chores. Then the pushing, shoving, and name-calling began. As my dad was about to pick up Dave and throw him against the dining room wall, I snapped!

I remember the details only vaguely, but my sister Jane recalls that I came at my father like a screaming warrior. I ran toward him yelling, "No more! No more! It's your turn, old man. It's your turn, old man." I grabbed him by the back of his shirt and pants and held him over my head. I turned him around so that all my siblings could see him. There he was, hanging in the air with fear and terror written all over his face. Then I threw him against the dining room wall. The whole house shook.

He lay there, shocked and frozen in fear. I had knocked the wind out of him. Shortly thereafter I walked up to him and with my finger in his face screamed, "Never again will you touch another person in this house, never again!" I walked out of the house and ran behind our garage. There I cried for hours until I fell asleep. Since that day, my dad has never touched us, yelled at us, or even spoken in a loud tone of voice. The reign of terror was over.

Jake's dad became passive and withdrawn after that day. Unfortunately, the abuse continued because Jake began to act out his anger and rage in ways reminiscent of his dad's. The day Jake picked up his seven-year-old-son and threw him against the dining room wall, Jake's wife gave him an ultimatum: "Get help or I'm leaving! There will be no more yelling, screaming, taunting, or hitting!"

The Holocaust Museum in Israel has a powerful dedication:

"What we don't learn from the past, we are destined to re-peat." Indeed, by the end of his story, Jake could hardly catch his breath. His face and his voice full of remorse, he admitted, "The moment I threw my dad against the wall, I became him."

Jake had promised himself never to be like his dad. Unfor-tunately, in such situations there are, I believe, often only two options: we become what we deny or we marry it! Many of us end up working for, living with, or entering into an intimate relationship with someone who is just like our mom or dad.

Unless Jake can learn how to embrace and lovingly accept what he hated in his father, he will become that unloved part of his father. He will repeat the patterns of anger and vio-lence. The vicious cycle of repeating the patterns of behavior from past generations in our own lives can be broken only with conscious acceptance and choice-making.

"Conscious acceptance" means a realization that I am the by-product of my mother and father. I am the finished and unfinished homework of their lives. What my parents have rec-onciled during their lifetime becomes my inheritance. What my parents have left unreconciled and ungrieved becomes my lifetime homework assignment. I carry within me various degrees of my parents' biology, psychological temperaments, dispositions, attitudes, customs, and traditions. The challenge of my lifetime will be to embrace all this favorable and unfavor-able potential. I need to accept personal responsibility for the choices that I make regarding the inheritance of my parents' healthy personalities and unhealthy pathologies.

Choice-making allows me either to repeat the past or to learn from it. Each of us can learn from our past and pass on to the next generation our collective wisdom. Or we can ignore the need for healing, reconciliation, and insight and pass on to the next generation our unfinished homework.

Since that day when Jake asked me to help him not become like his father, I have been gathering data from other men who share his concern. I have come to realize that so many men re-peat the past because they have no one to teach them new ways of male parenting or fathering.

The Importance of Fathering

Distortions and myths shape most men's images of their fathers. These images are based on the uneasy, peripheral place that fathers occupy in their own homes. Boys grow into men with a wounded father image within. They develop a conflicting inner sense of masculinity that is rooted in their experience of their father as rejecting, incompetent, or absent.[1] Such a situation places great pressure on a growing son as well as on his father. Boys too often misidentify with their "wounded" father and thus cripple their own identity as men.

Lewis Yablonsky notes that a son's identification with his father's role and his acceptance of his father's message depend on several factors:

1. whether the son has a genuine affection for his father;

2. whether the father is delivering his message to his son from a podium of professional, personal, and emotional success;

3. whether his relationship to his father is intimate and emotionally intense; and

4. whether other important people in his life (notably his mother) encourage the boy to accept his father as a model.

If all of these conditions prevail, a son is more apt to be accepting of his father's message, and his life will, therefore, be more deeply affected by his father.[2]

One of the most significant influences on a father's style with his son is the imprint of his own father's style of parenting. It is consciously and unconsciously a factor that is always at work. Many men discipline their sons, counsel them, and "love" them in the same way as their own fathers did.[3] Men need to ponder and consider just what it is that they have learned from their fathers about fathering. There seems little doubt that the imprint left on a son from his father's style of fathering, his father's unique personality, and other social and family influences develop a boy's future fathering style.

Although sex roles are changing, Yablonsky contends that *fathers* are the primary transmitters of the basic rules of the society to their sons because they are more likely than mothers to be involved with the larger society. Boys tend to be heavily involved emotionally with their fathers as role models, even though they spend more time with their mothers, sisters, and peers. Boys look to their fathers for cues about how to act out their male roles and, specifically, their future roles as fathers.[4]

The father is a significant player in his son's ability to detach from his mother. The father-son interaction allows the son to adopt a male identity and to explore the male's world. "The father helps the child disentangle his/her ego from the mother's through creative interaction and play. The father is the first stranger and representative of the outside world and can be viewed as a persecuting intruder or as a strong and friendly supportive hand."[5]

Samuel Osherson reminds us that the boy is searching deeply throughout his childhood, beginning around age three, for a masculine model on which to build his sense of self.[6] Research evidence shows that between the ages of three and five, boys begin to withdraw from mothers and feminine ways and become quite stereotyped and dichotomized in their thinking about what it means to be "like Daddy" and "like Mommy." Little boys begin to segregate by sex, to focus on rules rather than relationships, and to emphasize games of power, strength, and achievement. Eventually, they repress their wishes to be held, taken care of, and cuddled, the wish "to burrow among women."

But much of the male behavior with which men in our society have had to identify cannot be viewed as healthy, truthful, and wholesomely masculine. Masculine expressions have been twisted and denigrated by commercialism, television, racism, chauvinism, prejudice, abusive religiosity, and cultural fanaticism.

One man who attended our men's group expressed this dilemma: "When I think of fathering, I keep seeing pictures of my mother. I struggle to see images of my dad or the dads of my friends. When I had questions about how to care for my infant son, I didn't call my dad for guidance. I had to talk with my mother." How do we help men claim their rightful place as fathers with their own style and expression as male parents? As men explore their domain of child-rearing and fathering, the practices, attitudes, parental role involvement, and role satisfaction need to be named and specified.[7]

Although I do believe that fathers and mothers share many common parenting expressions and traits, I do not believe this means that men must continually conform to mothering behaviors. Emotions are universal; emotional expressions are typical of the human condition. However, the very biology of a male will determine and condition his expressions of affection, care, concern, warmth, and strength. A man does not have to emasculate himself nor reduce his masculine expressions to justify his male instincts or his fathering style.

Much still needs to be said about the value and goodness of a man's paternal power, expression, and authority. Unfortunately, the difficulty of finding role models for healthy male paternal behaviors may deter us from the opportunity to learn the skills first hand. We may have to borrow from other male role models in order to enhance our options and possibilities.

The Absent Father

If the implications of having an unhealthy father role model can be so devastating, is it possible that a father's absence is to be preferred? Research concerning fathering and its impact on younger males confirms the theory that the absence of fathers and inactive parenting of fathers have negative consequences on their sons' psychological, intellectual, spiritual, sociological, sexual, moral, and ethical development.

Michael Lamb provides a wonderful review of the range of issues involved in the role of the father in child development and implications of the father's absence on the development of a son. Boys raised without a father are reported to be less masculine in regard to sex-role preference and behavior. If the father is absent physically and/or emotionally during the primary years of a boy's life (from one to seven), a boy may struggle the rest of his life with an inability to form attachments, bonding, or emotional trust.[8]

The literature indicates that delinquents are more likely to come from father-absent homes. Some studies have shown that delinquent sons often come from homes where the father is antisocial, unempathetic, and hostile. Another research project determined that poor father-child relationships were common antecedents of delinquency, even when there were apparently normal mother-child relationships. It appears that the effects of low identification with fathers who are present are quite similar though somewhat less pronounced than the effects of fathers who are absent.

Further studies show that the correlation between paternal nurturance and the child's intellectual functioning is higher for boys than girls. There is a good deal of evidence that the father may exercise a strong influence over his son's intellectual development.

Paternal encouragement has a correlation with achievement. Underachieving boys have inadequate relationships with their fathers, whom they regard as rejecting or hostile. High achieving boys want to be with their fathers more than low achievers do, and they perceive themselves as more like their fathers. A close father-child relationship and the characterization of the father as both dominant and democratic are associated with high achievement and motivation in both boys and girls, but particularly in boys. One of the more consistently reported effects of a father's absence on sons is a deterioration of school performance and intellectual capacity.[9]

A father's warmth is correlated with a boy's feeling of self-esteem. Paternal nurturance helps the son with personality adjustment and self-confidence. Many studies report that the quality of the relationship between father and son is perhaps more important than the father's punitiveness or masculinity. The significant factor seems to be the father's relational importance in the child's life rather than particular techniques the father uses in dealing with his child.

One of the best established findings is that the masculinity of sons and the femininity of daughters are greatest when fathers are nurturant and participate extensively in child-rearing. This association depends, however, on the fathers' having sufficient interaction with their children. Therefore, the extent of the father's commitment in child-rearing is crucial. The father's similarity to a caricatured stereotype of masculinity is far less influential than his involvement in what are often portrayed as female activities.[10]

In their book *King, Warrior, Magician, Lover*, Robert Moore and Douglas Gillette note that the disappearance of the father through either emotional or physical abandonment, or both, wreaks psychological devastation on children of both sexes. The weak or absent father cripples both his daughter's and his son's ability to achieve their own gender identity and to relate in an intimate and positive way with members both of their own sex and the opposite sex.[11]

In *Finding Our Fathers*, Samuel Osherson states that the psychological or physical absence of fathers from their families is one of the greatest and most underestimated tragedies of our times. He goes on to say that if the father is not there to provide a confident, rich model of manhood for his son, then the boy is left in a vulnerable position: having to distance himself from his mother without a clear and understandable model of male gender upon which to base his emerging identity. Such a conflict can create in a young boy the inability to deal with personal authority and relationships to outside authority.[12]

Finally, Leonard LeSourd notes the correlation between a father's absence from the home and a higher delinquency rate, more premarital pregnancies, lower school performance, and greater drug use in his children.[13]

Expectations

In a brief report of women's expectations of men's behavior in the transition to parenthood, a pilot study of thirteen women undergoing the transition to motherhood indicates that women's expectations, men's promises, and media images of fatherhood did not coincide with the actual behaviors of fathers. This fact caused and amplified stress in the relationship. Many men supported the idea of becoming a parent but allowed their partners to have unrealistic ideas about the degree to which they would engage in active parenting. Counseling psychologists often focus on the woman's involvement with the baby or lack of partner support as the main problem in the couple's well-being. However, the mismatch between changing attitudes toward fathering and the impact of the consequent, apparently false expectations regarding men's behavior in the early years of parenthood may also have a significant impact on the couple's relationship.[14]

Expectations of how a man provides fathering or active parenting, caretaking, and overall involvement with his children cause clashes between men and women as long as women provide the definitions and men fail to rise to the occasion. Men need to clarify through their own male experiences and particular masculine expressions how they will father, parent, and provide child care. Unfortunately, defining how a man provides nurturance is not an easy job. Kyle Pruett asks:

> Why is it so hard for our society to acknowledge fathering as a truly vital issue? Why do so many of the men we will meet [in his book] feel so lonely, isolated, even excluded and ridiculed by friends, and occasionally family for giving their parental role such seminal importance in their lives? Why is it so hard to take such men and their children seriously? Are we truly that much more comfortable as a society with the image of the "Life with Father" despot, who reigns benevolently over his family but in truth has little if any nurturing power or authority beyond administration? We accept images of skillful executives and bureaucrats, providers, entertainers, protectors — but not down-to-earth, flesh-and-blood nurturers.[15]

The underground father is struggling his way out of the catacombs and into the daylight, elbowing and bellycrawling under and around the barbed wire of the old masculine stereotypes. He knows it may yet be possible to be emotional and vulnerable enough to nurture without feeling or looking like a victim. An interesting indicator of this change in attitude is the fact that the 1985 Yale graduating class asked retired Senator Paul Tsongas of Massachusetts to address it on its Class Day. He is a hero who is "not a minion of Wall Street, the playing fields, the theater of war, Madison Avenue, the Oval Office, Hollywood, or Broadway — he is a father facing a fatal illness who decided to go home to his family."[16]

The vital challenge to be embraced by men will be their ability to redefine their concepts of male, father, and fathering to include masculine emotion, affective expressions, and appropriate rituals. Men will be able to relate to their children in an emotionally expressive, sensitive, and spontaneous manner only if they are able to view these behaviors as consistent with their conception of male sex role standards.[17]

Part One

THE WOUNDED MALE
AS FATHER

Five Unhealthy Fathering Styles

FIVE UNHEALTHY FATHERING STYLES

	DICTATOR	TRICKSTER	COMPETITOR	MAGICIAN	VILLAIN
Primary Expressions	Passive-aggressive behavior, Rage, Indifference, Moral imperatives	Sarcasm, Belittling, Debasing, Humor	Defensiveness, Sabotage, Caution	Chameleon, Adapter, Coldness, Aloofness, Arrogance	Pity, Shame, Violence, Domination
Personal Fear	Loss of control, To be revealed	Loss of safety, To become vulnerable	Loss of attention and audience, To be weak and needy	Loss of invisibility, To be unable to escape	Loss of power, To be victimized
Primary Vice	Anger	Fear	Anxiety	Projection	Revenge
Delusional Idea	I am all-powerful	I am entitled	I am without fault	I am not responsible	I am justified
Relational Style	Dependence, Self-centeredness, Withholding	Constriction, Insulation, Isolation, Slipperiness	Conditional acceptance, Task-orientation	Tentativeness, Provisional, Belonging, Avoidance	To use or be abused, Top-dog, Exclusiveness
Dominant Fathering Qualities	Male dominance, Hostility, Exaggeration, Guilt, Verbal abuse	Fear of relationships, False sense of potency, Boyishness, Immaturity, Temper tantrums	Annihilation, Alienation, Competition, Perfectionism	Addictions, Evil, Denial, Deceit, Delusions	Exploiting weakness, Sexual, verbal, and physical abuse, Victimization, Explosiveness

As you read about the fathering styles that are harmful and detrimental, it may become clear to you that your father practiced one or more of these unhealthy fathering styles. You may notice bits and pieces fitting into your depiction of your father or even of yourself.

Each of us can act out some or all of the five unhealthy fathering styles. But because we are creatures of habit, we usually specialize. Each of these fathering styles reflects a unique and particular way of relating and coping with human relationships.

Believe in your hidden stories and unspoken secrets. You may find yourself in great pain while reading these chapters. Take time out to be with someone who can be with you in your pain. Don't fall prey to the lie that "keeping it to myself will make it more manageable." Memories, dreams, and recollections will occur as you read these chapters. You may also discover your need to release your rage. You may want to make a gesture of forgiveness or prepare a rite of reconciliation with your father.

Chapter 1

THE DICTATOR FATHER

— ✥ —

Fathers, do not provoke your children to anger; but bring them up with the training and instruction of the Lord.

—Ephesians 6:4

* *I was the youngest of six children. I watched my father drive each of my brothers and sisters away because of his anger and rage. Each of my siblings escaped the home; we still suffer the wounds of anger inflicted by our father.*

* *"It's my way or the highway" was my dad's favorite line. We never talked at the dinner table. Any discussion ended with my dad's last words. I never had a sense that what I said was important or that it mattered.*

* *I lived my whole life waiting for his approval. I lived my whole life according to all his moral dictates. His directions always included, you "should," "ought to," "must," "have to," and "never," "ever," or "always." Today, I'm not sure of anything. Now I struggle to believe that I even have a choice in life.*

* *I can remember my high school all-state basketball game. I was first string and played center position. I can still hear my old man screaming at me. He belittled me for any error or mistake I made. I remember once that someone tripped me and I slammed against the floor real hard. I looked up and there was my father yelling at me to kill the guy who tripped me. The only person I wanted to kill was him.*

◆ *Children should be invisible and not heard or seen. My father ruled the house with his mood swings. If he laughed, we all began to relax. If he came home angry, we hid. If we weren't sure of his mood, we tiptoed around just waiting to see who and what would set him off.*

Primary Expressions

The dictator father rules the household with an iron fist. He makes no concessions for error and lacks patience with his son. Rules are moral absolutes. There is no room for balanced direction that helps a young man come into his own sense of right and wrong. The parent role is very rigid. The son lacks the ability to wonder, doubt, question, and ponder his place in the family relationships. There is little or no dialogue in this kind of father-son relationship. Dictatorial declarations, subtle tensions, and discomfort fill the silence between father and son.

◆ *"Either my way or no way" was the rule of the house with my dad. He never lived what he expected us to live. He was full of contradictions. We had to fulfill his ideals while he lived by another set of rules. Even today, I struggle with anyone who tries to tell me or show me any kind of direction. I guess I'm still fighting my dad.*

◆ *I remember working in my father's grocery store. One day a customer returned with his receipt. He had paid too much for his merchandise. I began to investigate when my father came rushing in on the scene. He began to yell and scream at me for making such a stupid mistake. He berated me for being slow and told me I was not worth the clothing on my back. The customer tried to interject. My father kept on pointing his finger at me. He talked loud enough so everyone in the store could hear him tear me apart. When I began to cry, he would then shout at me that I was just a spineless sissy. Then came all the degrading names: queer, fairy, little girl Jamie (my real name is James). Finally, the customer got a word in and declared loud enough to be heard over my father's big mouth, "Excuse me, sir, it wasn't your son who waited on me; it was you!" I don't remember what happened after that mo-*

ment. *I never heard my father say, "I'm sorry," or admit making a mistake. He never admitted to any error.*

The dictator father misuses power and authority. He struggles with any personal self-disclosure. The verbal abuse from the dictator father strangles and emasculates his son, creating a fearful and dependent relationship. Because discipline may lack purpose and meaning, his son will lack personal awareness of choices, imagination, risk-taking, and exploration. This father role typically reflects a fear of his son. It is as though the father must oppress his son or his son will escape from bondage.

The dictator father generates confusion and mistrust by his silence and moodiness. The father's indifference to his son's achievements creates an empty space for the son. The son never feels as though he has bonded with or wants to emulate his father.

- *My mom always came to the awards night at our high school. Each of her five kids would win some special award for art, science, music, or sports. I wanted my dad to be there, but it just wasn't worth putting up with his criticisms. He would find some fault with what we did or didn't do. It was never any fun having him around.*

Personal Fear

The dictator father does his best not to be revealed. He covers up any exposure to his inner world of personal thoughts and feelings. He is captive to his own world of moral imperatives. Anyone who comes to know him feels a tension created by his rigidity and inability to let others into his space.

- *I always wanted to know what my dad was so afraid of. It seemed as though he was always looking over his shoulder. He never had any friends. I don't remember my dad hanging out with anyone, including our relatives. Our relatives didn't like him. He had an imperial attitude. I still remember my Uncle John saying about my dad: "He may not be right, but he is never wrong."*

Control is a primary preoccupation with the dictator father. His need to be all-knowing and in charge takes up most of his attention. The movement of the family and its routines are all determined by what the dictator father desires. His desires may also change rapidly. The family continues to adapt to his changing needs by putting father before anyone else.

This obsession for control dominates the relationship between father and son. This undermines the son's ability to learn from his father's personal experiences. He also lacks the collected wisdom of masculine usage of control, discipline, and authority.

- *I watched my father slowly die of cancer. Even in his weakest moments he still had to be in charge. He was calling the shots to the last breath. I watched my mother and sisters attend to his every beck and call. I remember being alone with him one day. He wanted me to change the TV channel. I was watching a documentary that would help me with a research paper, a final project. The paper was due in two days. My time away from college came at a great personal sacrifice, but I was determined to do much of my work at home. I didn't want to lose out on completing this semester. Again my dad demanded that I hand over the remote control to him so he could watch what he wanted. I held on to it and we struggled for a few moments. I finally jerked it out of his hand and startled him by my forcefulness. I looked him straight in the eyes and I said, "I gave up my whole life to please you and do what you wanted. You can sit your ass in bed and sacrifice a few moments of your precious time. I don't give a shit what you want. It's my turn." I turned up the volume of the documentary and sat there with lots of anger and disappointment. After the documentary was over, I tossed the remote control onto his bed and walked out.*

Primary Vice

- *As a small child I can remember crying a lot when my dad would talk to me. I always thought he was yelling at me. My mom would reassure me that he was hard of hearing and had to talk loudly. Later on in my childhood, I came to see that my mom was covering up for my dad. He wasn't hard of hearing; he was yelling at me and everyone he spoke to. I remember when I was with my softball team. We were practicing, and my dad, sitting in the bleachers, began to yell at my teammates. He was calling out all kinds of instructions and criticisms. My teammates asked me, "Why is your dad always so angry?" The coach went over to ask my dad to stop yelling at the team. He walked away after that. When I got home, he told me that I couldn't play ball anymore. From that day on, I never did.*

Aggression, rage, criticism, name-calling, verbal abuse, and violent body gestures and are but a few of the tactics used by the dictator father. He is insecure with his own sense of self and lacks inner confidence. The dictator father offsets his insecurity by dominating others, especially his son. This father style demands respect from his son. Unfortunately, fear, not respect, is bred in this relationship. There is no personal exchange. The father withholds most personal affection from his son. It is typical that the son of a dictator father has no memories of being hugged, touched affectionately, or embraced by his father.

The dictator father repeats the sins of *his* father. He also was oppressed and not lovingly parented. He passes on to his son this same deprivation of personal affection. Life becomes a series of injustices. Trust no one! Keep up your defensive posture so that you won't be ripped off. This is the ongoing message of the dictator father.

Delusional Idea

The dictator father feeds his delusional thinking with the belief that he is all-powerful. He exempts himself from observing norms of ethics and morality. He places himself above the law and is rigid and vicious in his application of the law to others. The dictator father believes he is invincible and infallible. When he is insecure, the dictator father uses a variety of strategies, such as passive-aggressive behavior, avoidance, aggression, dominance, exhibitionism, sensationalism, and verbal abuse.

A good example of the dictator father can be seen in the movie *The Great Santini*. Bull Meechum is a marine air pilot who dominates his family and treats them like a drill sergeant working his platoon. The movie begins with Bull's wife and children waiting for his arrival at an air force base. Lillian, Bull's wife, has the children dressed and ready for her husband's inspection. She instructs her children as Bull's plane lands, "Okay, children, stand in line. He'll probably hold inspection when he comes. Stand up straight, Ben. You know he'll be on you about that.... Girls, check your hair. Remember, walk, walk to meet him. I'll give him a big juicy. The girls will give him a big juicy and you boys shake hands firmly, very firmly and say, 'Welcome home, Colonel!' " Later, Bull has his children lined up on the front porch. He says to them in a condescending voice, "Okay, hogs! I've heard you belly-aching about moving to this new location." He continues to berate them and to dictate terms of expected behavior. He treats the children as he would a company of soldiers.

When his military strategies don't work, Bull begins a tyrannical string of verbal abuse. He berates his children by calling them derogatory names: hogs, homos, fags, jockos, etc. Throughout the movie, we come to see how one man takes the spotlight unto himself and treats everyone else as second-best. It is not unusual that the dictator father establishes routines and rituals that fit his own personal temperament while he expects the rest of the family to adjust according to his needs. The routines of a dictator father are often carried over into the next generation because those who have survived living with a dictator father have not learned other options to draw upon for parental nurturing.

Another scene in this movie shows the family driving for hours to their new home. The morning after they have arrived in their new house, Bull wakes the whole family early in order to keep his personal schedule and expectations in line for the day. He shows no concern that the family is exhausted from traveling and anxious about the move to a new location. On another occasion, he awakens his son Ben at 4:00

a.m. to give him a birthday present. Bull hands the boy the air force jacket he had worn during World War II. Ben is barely awake when he is given his father's gift. The dictator father is more impressed with himself and his supposedly magnanimous generosity than with the impact this has on his sleepy and slightly confused son.

In another scene Bull is driving and awakens Ben, who had been sleeping beside him. They begin to talk on a personal level. Ben tries to tell his father some of his fears and concerns about college. He says, "What if I decide I don't go into the Marines, Dad?" His father answers very emphatically, "You're going in! Four years after college, you can decide what you do after that. You're going in!"

The dictator father is convinced that he has an inside track on what's best for everyone. He is unable to understand or to judge anyone else's behaviors outside of his own personal expectations, definitions, and beliefs. Those under his guidance will be expected to mold themselves into the dictator father's style of thinking, feeling, and behaving. The dictator father's pronouncements and decisions are to be considered as absolute moral imperatives.

Relational Style

◆ *I listen to my friends talk about their dads and recount personal stories about their dads' lives. I have no point of reference. I know nothing about my dad. All I know about him is a vague description of a person who I lived with for eighteen years. He has no personal features or characteristics that I can talk about. He was cold, aloof, and demanding. He came home from work and lived his own life. We were to be on duty from the moment he walked into the house. We were expected to respond with undivided attention to meet his pleasures. I don't know what kind of ice cream he liked or if he had fun as a kid. I don't know about my dad's past or his dreams. I have a big empty space in my chest when I try to feel love or affection for him. I know in my head that I should love my father. He did bring me into this world and fed, clothed, and housed me. Yet I have such an indifferent feeling toward him. In fact, I have no*

feeling at all. I can't say I hate my father. I just don't know how to
love someone who feels like a stranger.

The dictator father depends on no one. He is self-serving. He creates a presence that leaves his children cold and wanting. His involvement with his son becomes duty-oriented. Fathering is a responsibility and an obligation. It is a task that the dictator father undertakes as a duty and fulfills through order and discipline.

◆ *My father treated me like his car. If anything got broken or hurt,*
you just fixed it so it could perform again. I had to be fed at a
certain time, whether I was hungry or not. I had to go to the toilet
upon his demand. It was expected that I accomplish certain tasks
at a certain age. I had to function and perform according to his
dictates.

Parenting for the dictator father is impersonal, formal, and based on accomplishing external goals. The dictator father considers personal feelings and others' emotions as unimportant and unacceptable. If the dictator father tries to help his son, he does it either by dominating the occasion or by manipulating the outcome to meet his expectations.

◆ *I have always had a love of building things. I was with my next*
door neighbor, and we wanted to build a tree house. Unfortunately,
my dad got news of our intent and came over to help. My dad
never really helped. He took over and did what he wanted to do.
As my dad dominated the construction of the small tree house, my
friend got disgusted and left. He got tired of being told that what
he was doing was wrong. I had to stay and put up with my new
role as servant and "go-fer" for my dad. Well, the tree house got
built; my dad did it all and did it his way. The next day my friend
and I had fun dismantling the tree house. It was the only thing I
could do right — tear the sucker down.

◆ *I have this voice in my head. It's my father. I hear him remind-*
ing me, even now at the age of twenty-three. "Jim," it seems to
say, "you have no rights, no options, no imagination. You're too

stupid and slow and don't matter anyway. You have no privileges, no ideas worth keeping, and don't even think your own thoughts. Feelings are a waste of time, so forget them. Just do what you are told to do. Don't ask why — just how, how much, how long, how many times, and how can I please you, Dad?" I want to get rid of this voice in my head. It has run my life long enough. I want to be in charge of my own life.

Dominant Fathering Qualities

The dictator father parents his son by misusing his male dominance at the expense of emotionally raping his son's integrity and dignity. The dictator father relies heavily upon exaggeration. He uses his dominance to convince his son that he has the right to demand and expect obedience. The dictator father uses guilt to persuade his son to accommodate his desires. He manipulates and demeans his son's self-worth. This happens because the dictator father himself lacks self-esteem and personal worth.

◆ *There was never a day that I could remember that I didn't imagine my father at the steering wheel of our family car. The rest of us in the back seat would hold our breath and anticipate his next move. I can still see how we were all afraid of his nasty mouth. His hostility toward life permeated our entire family life. I always wanted to know why he was so angry at life. I wondered why he was so frightened by the unknown and unfamiliar.*

◆ *We nicknamed my father "Commander Chief." We used to say to one another as siblings, "We live for his pleasure." There was no question as to who was head of the household. The sad fact was that the "Commander Chief" had our attention, but not our affection. I remember when he died. There were no tears. It was a distinct feeling of relief. He would no longer try to undermine us or to argue with us. We no longer had to hide our thoughts and feelings from one another. We could think and talk without fear of criticism. We could relax with one another. If only my dad knew how much of life, loving, and living he missed out on.*

- *My family would get together on Sunday afternoons and play various games. Our time together was always more fun when my dad had to work on Sundays. When he didn't have to work, I noticed that we laughed less and became more serious. The day usually got heavy and tense if my dad was in one of his moods. He would start to nag about his work and then about the family. Then he would start with his routine about what we did wrong in playing the game. Sometimes he would end the game because we weren't playing it correctly. The game would end abruptly because he decided that we needed to do house chores or some stupid thing like that. I don't remember having fun with my dad. I wished many times that he would go to work and never come back. Even today, I don't like to play games. I just stay away from him so that I don't get mad.*

- *As I grew older, I realized that my dad had a split personality. At work, he was passive and had a "no-name job," as he described it. He made up for his lack of power and control at work when he came home. He decided everything. He tried to look big and important at home with his booming voice and dictatorial gestures. Later in life, I began to understand my father's behavior. His bark didn't match his bite. My dad was a weak and powerless man. In my early childhood, I thought he had authority and strength. Around age fourteen, I began to realize that my dad was a bag of wind. I learned to accommodate his demands, but had no respect for him. Today, my dad tries his bellows to see if I'm paying attention. Sometimes it works, but most of the time I just ignore him. We don't have a relationship. I tolerate him. He, in turn, tries to flex his muscle by being mouthy and dictatorial. I'm not sure who is the neediest between the two of us.*

The dictator father hides behind his facial gesture, tone of voice, and physical posture. He tries to communicate power and authority by misusing control and strength. Rules, laws, and principles are abused for the sake of gaining control. Disciplines are inappropriate. Discipline is meted out to convince his son of parental power and position. Punishments often do not match the crime. If anything, the wrongdoing is remembered. Then the remembered event is used for the future disciplinary actions.

The son of a dictator father lives around his father. The son lives with a sense of caution, tentativeness, and hesitancy in this father-son relationship.

Chapter 2

THE TRICKSTER FATHER

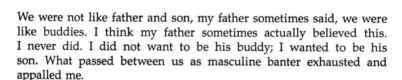

We were not like father and son, my father sometimes said, we were like buddies. I think my father sometimes actually believed this. I never did. I did not want to be his buddy; I wanted to be his son. What passed between us as masculine banter exhausted and appalled me.

—James Baldwin, *To Be a Man*

♦ *My mother would say that she had four children. Her first son was her husband, and then she had three other children. I never perceived my dad as an adult. He was always hiding behind my mother's skirt. When he did try to act like an adult, it would take just a little conflict and off he would go to hide. His favorite hiding place was to blame someone else.*

♦ *If you wanted a prototype of a con artist, you would want to meet my dad. He could sell ice to an Eskimo and convince him that he should be grateful for all he did. My dad taught me how to deceive others. He was an expert at it.*

♦ *Empty promises and false hopes would begin to describe how I feel about my dad. He would promise to meet me at my baseball games and would never show up. His favorite line was, "I'll make it up to you someday, son." Well, so far that someday hasn't happened. Even today he promises to come to dinner and never shows up. I've learned not to wait, but I do still hope that someday he will come through for me.*

◆ *Frank, my dad, was liked by everybody. He was a great storyteller, had funny jokes to share all the time, and was the life of the party. However, when talking to him just don't use the words "sacrifice," "commitment," or "dependable." Frank was nothing more than a funny bone, a pathological clown. I don't like to laugh anymore. I guess it's because I don't trust humor or laughter.*

◆ *I'm a very insecure kind of guy. I spent most of my life being teased and taunted by my dad. I never figured out where I stood with him. He would hide behind his jokes. I remember riding my bike one day when I fell and broke my arm. On the way to the hospital, all that my dad did was to talk about how funny I looked when he found me. Then, he reminded me of all his broken bones and that mine wasn't that bad.*

Primary Expressions

The trickster father elevates himself at the expense of debasing others. He is slippery, deceitful, and dramatic when it becomes useful for him in order to get what he wants. He can be grandiose in his perceptions and make promises that will not be fulfilled. These broken promises multiply over the years. Finally, the son of a trickster father becomes aware of his father's inability to care for anyone except himself.

◆ *Give my dad a few drinks and watch out. Here comes Bozo the clown! He would do anything, say anything, and use anybody to get people to laugh at him. He would belittle me and use me as the brunt of his jokes. All the guys he would hang out with laughed at me. I knew they realized that if they didn't, they would be the next victim for my dad's teasing and joking.*

The self-serving behavior of the trickster father eliminates any parental role that he may have with his son. The son of a trickster father can pinpoint the time in his life when he realized that he had outgrown his father's poor behavior. The roles of father and son are either abolished or reversed. At this point, the son may begin to parent his father and take on adult responsibilities prematurely.

◆ *I remember at the age of five that I was sent to go and get my father from the bar. This went on for years. At the age of nine, I realized that I had become my father's babysitter. He would remind me to pick him up at the bar around 4:00 p.m. so he could be home before dinner. One day I forgot to go to the bar to get him. He came home late that night enraged at me. He said that I made him miss dinner because I didn't come to get him from the bar.*

◆ *My dad would always complain if my mother asked him to do any-thing. His favorite response was, "Have you asked Tom, your son, to do it?" Everything was measured in equal proportions between my dad and me. Later in life, I realized that he was no one I would look up to with respect. I resent the fact that, as I grew up, I had an "older brother" who was supposed to be my father. All I ever learned from him was how to complain and to escape from work and responsibility.*

The trickster father acts like an immature adolescent. He seems to have little control over his emotions. He cries and whimpers for the sake of getting what he wants. He can act like a wounded animal until someone concedes to his wants, and then he turns into a waiting viper. Most of all, the trickster father wants his son to make up to him for all life's troubles and burdens. The son is dispensable for the sake of the father's pleasures.

There seems to be little or no self-abasement or self-reproach in the trickster father when he causes harm to another person. He humiliates, embarrasses, shames, and dupes his son with the hope that he, the father, will achieve a personal goal.

The son of a trickster father learns at an early stage in life not to depend upon his father. If the son's need fits into the desires of a trickster father, then the son might get some leftover time and attention from his father.

◆ *My dad began an interest in bowling during my senior year in high school. He would meet me and my friends at the bowling lanes every afternoon in order to practice. I thought he was there to support me and that he wanted me to excel in my new hobby. After a few weeks, I saw him flirting with one of my female classmates.*

Then they left the bowling alley and didn't come back. My friends began to tease me about my dad "playing the field" at his age. I was mortified and angry. I had other experiences like this with my dad. I felt cheap. I felt like I was a pimp for my dad. When I began to confront him about his behavior, he "buddied" up to me and said that we were pals. He would make light of my embarrassment and say to me, "You know, son, boys will be boys."

Personal Fear

A primary concern of the trickster father is to develop a safe place to get his needs met without consequence to himself. He fears becoming vulnerable and dependent upon anyone. His affections are plentiful as long as it doesn't cause him any pain or inconvenience. The trickster father's need for personal security and safety might require hurting another person or taking advantage of others. His need for autonomy and self-sufficiency is really a cover-up for his codependent condition. He lives off others. His strength is found in his ability to take advantage of those around him.

- *My father would never ask for help. If he couldn't do it by himself and for himself, it wouldn't get done. He taught me to hide whatever I didn't know. If I didn't know how to do something, he taught me to fake it. His motto was, "Don't let anyone know that you have a need." He taught me well. Before I got into a recovery program, I had no friends. I couldn't hold down a job and I had an arrogance about me that drove me into complete social isolation. I remember that in therapy my counselor asked me whose voice I heard telling me not to reach out for help. Like a lightning bolt, I screamed, "It's my father. He doesn't want me to ask others for help. I will hurt if I open myself up to you or to others."*

A false sense of self-reliance and self-dependency is modeled by the trickster father. In the father-son relationship there is a tension between what is real and what is a lie. The trickster father paints a false sense of reality for his son. Therefore, the son learns not to trust his perceptions, his environment, or his feelings.

Unable to learn from his father how to become vulnerable with others, the son of a trickster father becomes either an isolated person or a permeable membrane. Not sure how to contain himself and yet remain open to others, the son will maintain a "fight or flight" stance toward most relationships.

Primary Vice

The trickster father hides behind deception, runs from conflict, scapegoats others for what is his own responsibility, blames others when found guilty, and lets his fear determine many of his choices. A favorite coping skill when he's combating life's challenges is escape. When faced with a commitment, the trickster father can be easily sidetracked by other interests.

* *My dad never had a backbone. He was afraid of his shadow. I remember him asking me to do things that he wouldn't do himself; something as simple as returning a box of broken glasses to the hardware store was a major event for him. He would wait in the car as I made the drop-off and exchange. He would pump me up with all kinds of compliments so that I would feel confident in doing his dirty work. Then, when I returned, he would brag about how well "we" got the job done.*

* *When my mom would catch my dad drinking, he would come up with some grandiose lie. One day he came limping into the house and talked about how he was mugged. His story was that a grocery store manager came out and saved him. Afterward, the store manager gave him some whiskey to drink in order to help take away the pain. If you ever need an excuse for anything or a good lie to cover up a mistake or a far-fetched story to fake somebody out, ask my dad. He's a specialist.*

* *We waited forty-five minutes before I finally said, "Let the wedding begin!" I found out later that my old man was engaged in a card game and was on a losing streak. He wanted to get his money back before he was willing to leave the game. He met us at the reception with a big smile and a bottle of champagne. If it wasn't for my new wife who begged me not to make a scene, I would have broken that bottle over his head.*

He acted like nothing happened. His way of making up for it was to say repeatedly, "I guess I'll have to watch the video and see what I missed." It has been three years and he hasn't watched the video. The bottle of champagne my dad brought to the reception is still unopened.

Even though fear dominates the trickster father, he will at times take risks that can be life-threatening to himself and to others. The inability to manage his fearfulness can take on forms of bizarre behavior and irrational decisions. Not concerned with the implications of such behavior, the trickster father can harm himself for the sake of entertainment.

• *My father would always pick us up late from school. We had a good thirty-minute ride home. He would tease us sometimes by driving recklessly and running off the pavement. Sometimes he would slam on the breaks and blame us kids for distracting him because of the noise in the car. One day when my sister begged him not to drive so fast through a busy intersection, he did his regular routine of mental torture and began to swerve the car. We hit a pothole on the edge of the pavement and the car tipped and rolled over. The ambulance came and my father did everything he could to make a scene about his pain. He kept cursing the city for not fixing the potholes that caused this unfortunate accident. I was bleeding pretty badly; my two sisters were more scared then physically hurt. My father was rolling all over the ground, faking his pain and screaming that he needed immediate medical attention. The ambulance driver looked at me and saw the deep cut in my arm. The medical team swept me away to the hospital.*

I never heard just what they did for dear old Dad. Later that evening, my mom came to get me from the hospital. No one ever talked about what really happened to cause the car to roll over. My dad tried to bring a lawsuit against the county road commissioner. It never amounted to anything. For years my dad talked about how he was permanently hurt and disabled because of that pothole on the side of the street. He still claims to be disabled and unable to work. No doctor has been able to confirm that any of his symptoms are real.

Delusional Idea

The movie *Voyage Round My Father,* with Lawrence Olivier and Alan Bates as father and son, gives a glimpse of the trickster father's style. In this movie there are no names given to the father, the mother, or the son. Only the son's wife, Elizabeth, is named. Throughout the movie, the father communicates with his son only through his wife. We see the father writing letters, using poetry, riddles, and literary quotes as he tries to converse with his son. The father is known as a master gardener and he is also a well-respected lawyer, but as a result of a head injury, he becomes blind. The mother and the son become his eyes. Even so, the father's blindness doesn't hinder his work as a lawyer. No one mentions the father's blindness. Everyone acts as if the father never lost his sight.

The father, however, avoids all contact with his neighbors. If someone comes to visit, he gets up quickly and walks away. At one point in the movie, we see the father, mother, son, and daughter-in-law sitting outside. Referring to her husband, Elizabeth says to her father-in-law, "You've never really said anything seriously to him. Nobody here says anything. They tell stories and make jokes. Something is happening." The son speaks up and says, "Elizabeth, it doesn't always *have* to be said." Elizabeth replies, "Sometimes, sometimes it has to!" The father gets up and begins to walk away. He says, "Well, what do you want to hear from me, hey! What words of wisdom?" Then he slowly walks back to the house.

This movie depicts the trickster father and his avoidance of all conflict. He keeps his thoughts and feelings guarded or he toys with his words and speak in riddles and stories. This leaves his son feeling insecure and uncertain. The trickster father keeps himself at a distance from others in order to have enough space for himself to escape if the situation demands. We also see in this movie how the son unfortunately becomes allied with his father's tactics.

Relational Style

The trickster father is immature in his ability to share and to care for his son. He either hides behind his son for protection against his own mistakes or he uses his son to achieve those things he feels incapable of accomplishing on his own. The father's emotional immaturity keeps him from exhibiting characteristics of stamina, endurance, perseverance, and commitment.

- *Everything my father did with me and for me had some kind of "deal" attached to it. I always ended up owing him more than what I thought had been part of the bargain. He had to get something in order to give something. Sometimes he would make a deal with me and I would carry out my part of the deal. He, however, would renege, claiming that I misunderstood the agreement. I learned to hate my father. I learned how to trick people and make them think that we were negotiating and bargaining when, in fact, I was just ripping them off. Boy, Dad, you taught me well.*

The trickster father tries to appear fun-loving and playful. His son, however, sees him as constricted and rigid. The father's emotional insulation against others prohibits closeness with his son. The trickster father creates an emotional isolation. In so doing, the son may not have the chance to access emotions particular to fathering that he can learn only from his dad. The son's sense of masculine identity, power, containment, self-discipline, stamina, and endurance may remain dormant because of the son's inability to connect and bond with his trickster father.

- *I wondered for years what it would be like to trust and depend on my dad. Who would I be if I could have had a father who was honest and real with me? What differences would I be able to embrace if my dad taught me how to endure the pains of life instead of how to avoid and hide from it? I'm sure there is a man inside of my father, but he must be asleep. Who will awaken the man inside of me?*

The trickster father is perceived as the boy-man. His thinking, feeling, and behaving are immature. The trickster father looks like an adult, but his inner mechanisms are more attuned to those of a young adolescent.

Dominant Fathering Qualities

One man in our group stated that people are to be used in order to gain what you want in life. He also believed that all relationships serve only one purpose: temporary relief from oneself. The trickster father fears relationships and yet learns to toy with them. He engages his son in various activities for his own personal gain and pleasure. The amount of time spent together as father and son is based on the rewards and demands of the father. A relationship between the trickster father and his son is often inconsistent and unstable. Consistency is avoided because it might communicate commitment or dependability by the trickster father.

Parental respect is demanded by the trickster father, but his false sense of potency weakens with conflict or stress. The trickster father is the first one to abandon a sinking ship.

His temper tantrums and bouts of crying, screaming, yelling, and begging are a means of monitoring his son's reactions. It is typical for the trickster father to brag about all his sacrificing and giving. Yet when checked against reality, little or nothing has ever been sacrificed.

- *His favorite statement was, "After all I have done for you." I believed this statement as a child. Then, when I was a teenager, I cried out to him, "What exactly have you done for me? Help me to see it." There was silence. My dad knew that I had called his bluff. The silence at the moment broke my heart and hardened what was left of it. I then realized that my father had lived off my feelings and emotions long enough. It was time for him to feed himself and stop living off me.*

The tentative and evasive terms "maybe," "someday," "one of these days" are typical promises made by the trickster father. As a result, the son is often left feeling inadequate and insecure. The trickster father treats his son as an inferior person because he himself feels inferior. The trickster father creates routines and rituals of avoidance, procrastination, withdrawal, flight, or blame based on a false sense of strength and safety because he is unable to access his true potential.

◆ *When I was in high school, my friends would ask if my father was my older brother. At first I thought it was special to have my dad thought of and known as my brother. But when I needed my dad to help me make decisions or to struggle with school problems, my dad would make light of my problems and make fun of me. In my senior year in high school I got a girl pregnant. Her parents came to the house to discuss what she and I would do concerning this pregnancy. My mom was shocked and hurt, and she cried through the entire conversation. My dad declared to my girlfriend's parents that it was my problem. If I made the problem, I could solve the problem. He walked out, declaring he had a tennis game to play. It was then that I realized my father was incapable of caring for me when I was hurting or in pain. He left me alone when I really needed a friend, a companion, an adult. I have never recovered from that experience. I still want and need an adult male who can be with me and help me to work through my thoughts and ideas. I hope I find someone like this someday.*

Chapter 3

THE COMPETITOR FATHER

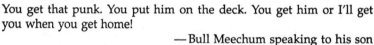

You get that punk. You put him on the deck. You get him or I'll get you when you get home!

> —Bull Meechum speaking to his son
> at a basketball game in *The Great Santini*

◆ *"Good, better, best, never let it rest!" That was my father's guidance throughout my life. I don't know how to relax or slow down or enjoy life. I have my father inside of me driving me eighty miles per hour.*

◆ *I tried to live my dad's unfulfilled dream of being a baseball player. I never really enjoyed the game. Since I can remember, all my dad would talk about was baseball. He would buy me magazines about baseball and take me to every game so I could learn to be the best. He never asked me if I ever had any fun. The day I stopped playing ball was the day my father started to nag me. We can't even talk without him reminding me what a disappointment I am to him. After all he did for me, just look at what I gave back to him.*

◆ *How do you ever measure up for a man who finds fault in everything you do? I spent my whole life adjusting to my father's criticism. I was never good enough, fast enough, or worked hard enough. I felt like I was never able to fit the bill. I only remember "more! faster! quicker!" —and only the flaws being pointed out.*

◆ *There was room for only one person in the spotlight, and that was reserved for my dad. I worked hard in high school and received a variety of awards for both academic and sports achievements. I always feared having my father come to these events. He would find some way to get the spotlight on himself. Before the evening was over, I would disappear and he would remain talking as though he had received some award.*

- *My dad took great delight in pointing out my faults. I can still see that sickening grin on his face when he could pounce on me or my brothers and sisters. I felt he was like a mountain cat waiting on some cliff for its prey to show any signs of weakness or a flaw. Then, he would begin with his driving, demanding, nagging criticisms. He would continue the mental torture until he had you crying. Then he would declare that he was right all along. We were just weak and stupid. "These aren't my kids," he would taunt. "They must belong to someone else."*

Primary Expressions

The competitor father is a chronic complainer. His own dissatisfaction with life is placed on the shoulders of his son. He finds fault and flaws with his son in order to avoid looking at himself and taking ownership of his own life choices. Blinded by his own eagerness and selfishness, the competitor father may try to live his own unachieved successes and victories through his son. The unhappiness of this type of father is projected on to his son. The competitor father lives with the false hope that he will get a second chance to achieve through his son. This second chance, however, may become a lethal expectation that affects the health and well-being of his son.

- *My father was a frustrated football player. He decided that his three sons — Tom, Joe, and me, Brad — would pick up where he left off. He also decided when we turned five years of age that he would begin to fatten us up so we could have an advantage for getting on our future high school football team. Do you know what it is like to be overweight because your dad thinks it's going to be to your advantage on some goddamn football team? I was the youngest of the three boys. My oldest brother would have panic attacks before a game. He got hurt a lot during games. Even if he hurt badly because of a game injury, my dad would take him in the back yard and point out all his mistakes. I can still see my brother limping while trying to keep up with my dad. It was times like these that I wanted to kill my father. My older brother had the good fortune to break his leg and could never play football again. He would sit next to my father in the bleachers during Joe's football games. While my dad was yelling and screaming and telling Joe everything he did wrong, Tom would sit silently. It was almost as if he weren't really there. Joe excelled in football, but my older brother and I were ignored. Every conversation at the table was about what Joe did or didn't do. I don't resent Joe for the attention he got. Sometimes, I feel grateful that my dad could put all his energies into Joe's potential career.*

As I got older, it was my turn to begin the tortures of my father's training and berating. One night while I was sleeping, I heard my brother Joe talking in his sleep. He kept calling for help. He was saying, "Daddy, help me. It's too big for me to carry. Help me a little or I'll die!" When I heard the word "die," something inside of me snapped. It was then that I decided I would not cooperate with my dad's demands for me to play football. Without telling anyone, I began to skip football practice. I was on the junior varsity team. It was to my advantage that Joe's team practiced on another field. Three weeks after no practice, my coach called my home and talked to my dad. When I came home that day, my father was mad as hell. He kept yelling at me and calling me some of his favorite four-letter words. I couldn't look him straight in the face. He kept yelling and screaming for what seemed like hours.

Soon after, the front door bell rang. It was Mr. and Mrs. Roberts, an older couple from next door. Mr. Roberts began to tell my dad that he could be heard all the way inside the Roberts's home. Mr. Roberts then informed my dad that if the yelling continued he would call the police. While he and my dad were arguing, I quietly slipped away.

I left that house at the age of fifteen and never returned. I believed in my heart that if I were to stay and live for my father's pleasure, I would die. I learned a lot about living on the streets. It was to my good fortune that I looked older than fifteen and could land a job and take care of myself. Today I work with street kids. I

*can understand why so many of them had to run away from home.
It's the only option I felt that I had to survive.*

The competitor father is easily blinded to the needs of his son. His own lust for satisfaction is fulfilled at a great price. His son must conform to his father's way of thinking, wanting, and behaving. In order to accommodate the competitor father, the son must sacrifice his own identity, self-worth, and personal dreams.

Personal Fear

The drive for success and attention is really based on the competitor father's fear of failure and loss. His inability to show weakness or need creates a false sense of strength and self-sufficiency. By indulging in masochism and a twisted sense of masculinity, the competitor father is incapable of being sensitive to the needs and the desires of his son. This particular fathering style creates relationships based on conquest and submission. His allies are usually other competitors who also want to dominate.

Personal friendship is absent in the competitor father. To be open to friendship would jeopardize his armor of invincibility. To advance as conqueror, the competitor father must continue his battles and defeat anyone who interferes with his goals.

A primary technique used by the competitor father to cover up his fear of failure is overestimation of his abilities. The competitor father brags about his unsung war stories. He exaggerates his experiences to make himself look godlike. No matter what his son does or accomplishes, the competitor father tries to surpass his son's successes. The competitor father resorts to sabotaging his son's achievements if he is unable to exceed his son's accomplishments.

By undermining or underestimating his son's accomplishments, the competitor father keeps such achievements at a mutual level with his own pseudoaccomplishments. The competitor father is unable to compliment or affirm his son; he seeks flaws in his son's performances or invents flaws to devalue his son's abilities.

- *I'm sure you've heard of the little boy who brings home his report card. He has earned five As and one B-plus. Then his old man bitches and complains about that one B-plus. Well, I would bring home a report card with all As and my old man would ask why they are not A-pluses. Or worse yet, he would say that I only got those As because of his genes and that I should be grateful for what he had done for me. Then he would go on and question my study habits, and who did I hang out with, and why didn't I spend more time helping my mother. It was a never-ending battle with that man. Today I am still driven and have a hard time enjoying my success. When I was in undergraduate school, I took a double major. When I went to graduate school, I took a double master's program. Now that I'm in doctoral studies, I'm not sure why I'm even here. I think I need to reassess what it is that I want. I guess my old man's questions and criticisms still charge me up and drive me around. I want to take charge of my life and live for myself for once.*

Some competitor fathers are less blatant in the abuse of their sons. They may be simply passive and indifferent toward their son's achievements. What is not spoken, however, can be just as wounding as what is said. When moments of success for the son call for celebration, joyfulness, or adulation, the silent presence of the competitor father can speak just as loudly as the spoken criticism. The competition for acceptance and acknowledgment between father and son results in the competitor father becoming unavailable, disinterested, busy, or preoccupied with choices that clearly state the father's preference for something or someone besides his son.

Primary Vice

- *My dad always seemed anxious and jittery. He couldn't stay in one place too long. He acted either bored or irritated. When he was in an unfamiliar situation, he would try to make jokes. He had a nervous laugh when he was in these situations.*

- *There was nothing subtle about my dad's need for attention. If he wasn't getting what he wanted, he would just steamroll his way through the situation until it ended the way he wanted. His inability to wait or to be patient was always a point of embarrassment. He would put himself before everyone. Something as simple as waiting in line at a grocery store could end up as a dramatic scene and embarrass the hell out of me. Of course, anyone in his way at the time was emotionally beaten up or mentally tortured by his sharp tongue.*

♦ *The last thing I would want to do is to ask my dad for any help. He was so pushy and insensitive. There was no room for error with him. He treated me as if I should have known how to do certain things all along. If I had any trouble with anything in my life, I would hide it so he wouldn't know about it. Keeping secrets from my dad became a way of life for me. To reveal any kind of neediness would just stir up trouble between us.*

♦ *He always wanted to be first. He had to eat first, leave the house first, be the first to win, the first to want and the first to get what he wanted. I can't remember any time when I saw my dad wait for something. He didn't wait for anyone or anything. He never let someone else go first. He had no idea what it meant to take turns. I learned at an early age that my dad was to be considered the most important part of our family. Everything else came after him.*

The competitor father is driven by anxiety. His restlessness permeates everything he does. He seems unable to enjoy the "here and now." Driven toward the next moment, he discounts what he has at any given moment and longs for what he might get. He is very demanding of himself and of those around him. Enough is never enough. He maintains a short-term sense of satisfaction and pleasure. His enjoyments are short-lived because of his drive for what will better provide what he really wants.

The competitor father maintains an inflated ego. He comes across as boisterous and gregarious while hoping that no one sees behind his mask. However, after a short time with the competitor father, one can see the exhibitionistic and self-centered person. He relates to his son by expounding on his own achievements, tasks, and accomplishments. He treats his son as a captive audience. The competitor father reprimands his son or deprives him of conditional acceptance if the son shows a lack of attention or admiration for his father.

Delusional Idea

"I am without fault" is the delusional idea of the competitor father. He maintains a stance in life that shields him from his own imperfections and weaknesses. He hides his vulnerability by competing for attention in every situation. He doesn't "play by the rules." Instead, he changes the rules of companionship to meet his own need to control. In *The Great Santini* we see the competitor father's style of parenting and the damage that this parenting style has on a son. Bull Meechum attends his son Ben's basketball game and shouts commands to his son from the bleachers. Ben is pushed by an opponent and knocked to the floor. Ben's father screams revengeful directions: "You get that punk. You put him on the deck. You get him or I'll get you when you get home!" We notice the embarrassment on Ben's face and we also notice the fear he has of his father's threat. Ben then deliberately pushes the opposing team player and the boy falls hard on the floor. The fallen opponent is carried off the court with a broken arm. Ben is suspended from the game and informed by the coach that he is dismissed from the team for playing rough. Ben's dilemma in this scene reveals the conflict between a competitor father and his son. The son is forced either to obey his father's inappropriate commands or to face his father's rejection and abuse. The competitor father teaches his son to always be on guard. He addresses his son with direct orders. His mandates leave no room for discussion. The competitor father issues directives to his son in an infallible and all-knowing manner. He ignores his son's feelings and comments. The competitor father evaluates situations from the standpoint of his own personal success, achievement, and victory.

Another scene from *The Great Santini* shows Ben and his father playing basketball in the back yard. The family is gathered around cheering for Ben, who reminds his father, "No one has ever beaten you in any game!" As Ben makes his victory shot and his family rallies around him, Ben's younger sister runs to her father to congratulate him even though he has lost. It's a dramatic and tragic scene. He yells at her and says, "Who the hell ever asked you? Get the hell out of here or I'll knock every freckle off your face!" Bull's wife, Lillian, tries to appease her husband, but he pushes her away. He stalks over to Ben and says, "You gotta beat me by two points. I changed my mind."

When Ben refuses to concede to his father's demands, Bull bounces the basketball off Ben's head and calls him "his favorite little girl." Ben just walks away. The rest of the family has already gone into hiding. The scene ends with Lillian and Ben looking out Ben's bedroom window. They are watching Bull shoot baskets in the dark in the pouring rain. Ben's mother assures him that his father isn't used to losing. She tries to convince Ben that it is hard for someone like Bull to lose to anyone. He is such a proud man.

The competitor father, like Bull Meechum, borrows some of the traits from the other four unhealthy fathering styles. We see that Bull is both the dictator and the competitor father. His personality also fits some of the characteristics of the villain father, evident in the closing scene. Bull comes home drunk one evening and begins to argue with Lillian. He pushes her around in the kitchen. The children hear them fighting and they quickly emerge from their bedrooms. As Bull wrestles with Lillian, Ben enters the room, grabs his father, and throws him against the refrigerator. Lillian cries out, "Get him! Get him!" Then each of the children join in on the attack. They all begin to beat on the father. Bull fights his way out of the attack and flees the house.

Relational Style

* *I got along well with my dad as long as I never had an opinion different from his. I learned to become an amoeba with him. Whatever he liked, I looked as though I liked it, too. If he didn't want something, neither did I. I realized by the time I was a teenager that*

I had become a xerox copy of my father. I became just as limited, scared, naive, and arrogant as my dad.

The competitor father tries to engulf his son and duplicates himself through his son's life and life choices. He compares his son's abilities with his own or with those of others whom the father admires. The father endlessly sets goals for his son, thus preventing his son from achieving his own goals.

The competitor father compliments his son only by bragging to his friends. Typically the son hears only from others that his dad has complimented and affirmed him.

◆ *I remember at my father's funeral that my Uncle John was telling me how proud my father was of me. In graphic detail, my uncle began to recount details of my success as a businessman, father, and husband. I was in so much pain as I heard these events about my life that I began to cry. My uncle assured me that all these kind thoughts and words came from my father. He told me that my dad was a proud man and thought that if he encouraged me too much he might make me weak. I blurted out to my uncle, "Encourage me too much! He never encouraged me at all. He never even acknowledged anything I did in my whole life. Having you tell me what my father thought and felt about me hurts me even more." I walked away from my uncle, who looked bewildered and perplexed. I spent days remembering what my uncle had shared with me about my dad's thoughts and feelings for me. I became so enraged that I thought I would burst. Why didn't my dad have the balls to tell me himself how he felt and what he thought about me? God, I wished he could have told me just one good thing about myself while he was alive.*

The competitor father lacks the ability to mete out care and concern in proportion to his son's needs. He may want his son to succeed and to achieve, but he has no sense of how to encourage his son without becoming pushy. He uses his own adult perceptions and personal measures to portion out what *he* believes his son needs. The competitor father lacks tolerance and sensitivity when his son resists. The competitor father perceives such resistance as a lack of gratitude.

The son of a competitor father wants desperately to get his father's approval and recognition. He may even adopt his father's expectations and strive to bring them to fulfillment. However, in an attempt to adopt his father's expectations, the son may be driven for the rest of his life to meet these goals, even to the point of physical and emotional harm or premature death.

A competitor father may ostracize his son if he abandons his father's expectations and strives to live his life according to his own personal pathway to excellence. The son may experience a great deal of tension and rejection from his father. The competitor father pits his own beliefs against his son's. The son becomes the enemy. The struggle between father and son becomes a battle of "conquer or be conquered." Unfortunately, most of the other family members become involved in this war between father and son as either allies or enemies of the competitor father.

- *My dad was your typical super-jock. He worked hard to look his best in front of others. He was known around the city as a real Don Juan. He had various affairs with women and didn't care who knew about them. I was nineteen years old when he was on his third marriage. It was at this time that I told him that I was gay. At first, he acted as though I were kidding. Then, when he realized that I was serious, he began to harass me. First, he blamed my mother because he thought she had treated me like a sissy. Then he blamed the private school that I had attended. He accused the school of being full of fags, anyway. Then he directly confronted me. I received the whole chorus of nicknames: "queer," "faggot," "prissy," and many others. Since that time, my dad and I haven't talked to one another too much. When we do get together, he is always telling gay jokes and making fun of my sexual preference. It's been hard to own up to my own sexuality. My dad has done nothing but add to the pain. I believe that if I could be just like him, we could be great pals; maybe even friends. But that will never happen now.*

Dominant Fathering Qualities

The competitor father is territorial. It is difficult for him to share with others, especially his son, with whom he competes for attention and recognition. As a father, he offers only conditional acceptance and affection. Many of these requisites must be purchased at a personal price by the son. If the competitor father offers any gestures of interest or concern for his son, they are usually followed by some condition to be met or by some requirement to be fulfilled.

> ♦ *My dad was quick to remind me of how much he did for me. Any time I was coaxed into covering up for his lies, it came with, "Remember such and such that I did for you?" I felt used by my dad. I was just one of many of his pawns. He had a way of making me feel that he did so much for me that now I owed him. I came to realize later in life that my dad was a "bleeder." He looked as if he had life all together. He could even fool most of the people with whom he worked. I can only remember giving, doing, and "putting out" for my dad. His needs always came first and anything left over was up for grabs.*

Learning how to develop a sense of your own space, personal expression, likes, and dislikes is important to developing a healthy sense of identity. The unfortunate result of being fathered by a competitor father is that personal space and a healthy sense of self are undermined for the sake of boosting Dad's ego. Some tragic results of the competitor father's influences on his son's growth and formation include loss of the son's self-esteem, weak ego-identity, and a deflated or inflated sense of sexuality.

Some young men live in the shadow of their competitor father's personality and become ineffectual with their masculinity. They assimilate their competitor father's characteristics. The son's ability to adapt to his father's wishes — thus losing his own identity — increases the psychic wounds already present.

Young men who rebel and try to live out their personal desires and goals independently of their competitor father's wishes do so at a great price to themselves. If, by chance, these men find others who will ally themselves with them and contribute to their struggle for independence and individual expression, they may break from the clutches of their father's domination. However, some young men will not survive these experiences because they have become powerless and ultimately will fall into despair and depression. Their identity takes on that of their competitor father.

The following story is an excerpt from a letter that was shared with members of a men's support group. The author's brother wanted us to know about this tragedy so that others, who may have had some of these same experiences, might come to realize that there are options when one is forced to cope with such personal pain.

Sam was the younger son of two children. His older brother, Steve, was a natural tennis player. The two of them had a lot of fun learning the game of tennis and competing together through various high school tournaments. Their father, however, was a former professional tennis player who lost his chance for big money and success because of alcoholism. Their dad was very bitter about his lost career and would compare anything the boys did in tennis to his once-successful career. The father ran a sporting goods store and still considered himself an expert tennis player. Sam writes the story.

- *I loved my brother, Steve. I realize now that he did his best to buffer me from the wrath of my dad. My dad had stopped drinking, but he never got into a recovery program. Even though he didn't drink like an alcoholic, he still talked and acted like one. I would hope and pray that he wouldn't come to our tennis games. When he did attend them, he would get all dressed up as though he were some movie star and sit in the bleachers with his dark sunglasses. Then his mouth would start. Every teammate learned to hate my father. No one was exempt from his vulgarity and arrogance. There were a few times when the authorities actually stopped the game and asked my father either to be quiet or to leave. My brother, Steve, did his best when he was out on those courts, but he always was aware of my dad's presence. I could see the strain on his face when my dad would correct him or call him one of my dad's favorite embarrassing names.*

When we got home after a tennis match, my dad would start in on us. Steve got most of the berating and belittling. I wanted to kill that man every time Steve would start to cry. No matter how well Steve played, my dad would find something he could correct. Even after Steve won a game, my dad would talk about how he would have won the game himself. My dad would stress that his way was the better way. You just couldn't win with that man.

When Steve was a senior in high school, I could see he wasn't coping very well with all the competition and with my dad's bitching and nagging. I woke up on October 4 and found a letter from my brother taped to my bedpost. He told me that he loved me and wanted me to forgive him. He wrote that he couldn't take the pressure, the criticisms, or the fact that he would never live up to my dad's expectations. He was sorry that he was such a failure in the eyes of my dad. Steve told me to be the best I could be and not to give in to what dad had to say about who I should be or what I should do. Finally, he signed the letter with, "Sorry, Sam. Love ya, Steve."

That same day my brother was found in the storage room of my dad's store. He had hung himself with a rope. He had attached a note for my dad that said, "I was already dead, but not yet gone. I'm no longer to blame, Dad. The only disappointment you'll find now is in yourself."

My brother tried to live a life more for my dad than himself. He tried to live the lie. The lie did him in. My father's anger at life killed my brother. I want everyone in the world to know that they don't have to live the lie for anyone. Don't live the lie or it will kill you.

The son who is unable to release himself from the unrealistic expectations of his father may live only to end his life in tragedy. The competitor father's desires and unfulfilled dreams may be fatal for his son. Even the father's best intentions for his son's life and future must be adjusted to meet his son's temperament and personal profile. In order for a competitor father to nurture his son properly, he must possess a level of "otherness" and sensitivity. Sadly, the competitor father who is caught up in his own woundedness may not be able to see beyond his own belly button.

Chapter 4

THE MAGICIAN FATHER

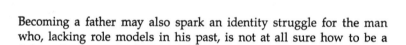

Becoming a father may also spark an identity struggle for the man who, lacking role models in his past, is not at all sure how to be a father who is present for his children.

—Samuel Osherson, *Finding Our Fathers*

♦ *When I was a young kid, I would ask my mom, "Who was that man that lived in our house for a few days and would leave?" My mom would remind me that he was my father. As I got older, I caught on to his routine. My father, the wandering idiot, would live with us until he got "the itch" to leave. Who knows where he went or what he did? He would leave some money to help pay for our expenses. One day he left and never came back.*

♦ *My dad was a slug who lived on the couch in front of the TV. His whole life consisted of going to work, coming home, and watching TV. The only time he spoke to us was when we might have eaten some of his junk food. Other than those occasions, he had nothing to say to us.*

♦ *The invisible man would best describe my dad. I lived at home until I was twenty-two years old. I can't remember my dad having any involvement with me. He just wasn't available. It was as though his body lived in our house, but his mind was elsewhere. I really don't know anything about my dad. I have no memories of me and him talking together.*

- *Everyone in my family learned not to ask any questions about my dad. He had absolute freedom to come and go with no strings attached. Yet, as if by magic, my dad was still in charge of the family. He would always speak through my mom. We kids never received any direction from him. As far as I'm concerned, his career was his first, and only, love.*

- *If passivity needed a second name, it would be Samuel, my dad. He could slip, unmarked, out of any situation. He was a master of manipulation. His ability to act indifferently in any situation drove my mom crazy. I think that's why I became such a daredevil. I tried everything I could to get his attention. I never understood just what that man wanted from me. Even today, I don't know how to get my dad's attention.*

Primary Expressions

The magician father is the most difficult to identify and describe of the five unhealthy fathering styles. Even though it is the most elusive style, there are some definite characteristics of this type of fathering that demand our attention. Men who compare their fathers to a "magician" unanimously agree that one feature each of their fathers shared in common is the ability to rule the household with some invisible force. The magician father covertly manages his position in the family by maintaining either a physical or emotional absence. He establishes a cynical detachment from his family while using passivity and indifference to insulate himself.

The magician father is perceived as secretive and elusive. His son may try to engage his attention by overcompensating with work and achievement, or he too might fall into patterns of passivity. Unable to become attached to his father, the son of a magician father struggles with feelings of self-esteem, belonging, attachment, and self-worth.

- *He would walk into the house and not say a word to anyone. I never really knew what the problem was. He would mumble and grumble about odds and ends, but I never heard him talk to anyone. I have always felt that my dad was possessed by some dark spirit. He looked oppressed. Being around him made me feel sad and burdened.*

♦ *My mom always encouraged us to respect our father. He provided us with a nice home, kept us well dressed, and put us through college. I was encouraged my whole life to honor and cherish a man I never got to know. He was invisible to me. I knew he worked hard to support us, but I don't know anything about my dad. My dad doesn't know anything about me, either. We never talked about personal things. I showed him my report cards and other awards I had won, but my dad doesn't know what I like or don't like. My head says he was a good worker, but my heart says he didn't give a damn. I would like to know why my dad lived his life in so much isolation. If he died today, I would grieve more for memories I don't have about my father than for his physical presence.*

Personal Fear

Even though the magician father maintains a high level of secrecy, he always has a connection with his family. That connection is his family's attention. It is necessary for the magician father to have this attention so that his shallow presence and his need to escape the family at any given moment will have an impact on the very people that he has come to ignore.

While maintaining his need for anonymity, the magician father does not want to be completely excluded or discounted by the family. He wants to be the one to ignore others or to determine who gets his attention. He is very good at creating a smokescreen behind which he hides his true feelings. He acts as if everything is fine so he can remain aloof and noninvolved.

The magician father's son either participates in his father's delusional thinking, or he must confront it. The son confronts his magician father by striving to share some personal need with him. Unfortunately, any demand for personal contact will send the magician father into an attack of cynical detachment or indifference. Although he may promise to give his son the time, attention, or affection, the magician father also sends confusing and ambiguous messages as to *how* and *when* he will fulfill these promises.

- *He would wait until the family was at a special moment, like someone's birthday or graduation. Then we would watch him bait us for his attention. He acted as though he were interested in the event. Just when we felt he was going to share in the moment, he would begin to criticize us. Then he would charm us out of our spotlight so he could get as much attention as possible. Once he had our attention, especially if we wanted more from him, he would get up and leave. I felt many times as if it were my fault that he left us because I asked him a question or wanted his affection. Later in life I realized his leaving was his way of saying, "I'll give you what I want to give you, and then I'm out of here."*

- *I considered my father an emotional addict. I never knew just what mood he would be in. One minute he would be smiling, then he would act as if he were possessed. When my father's moods kicked in, the whole family suffered from his dark self. It was as if we lived most of our lives under his black magic. When he wanted attention, it was at our expense. When he wanted to be left alone, it was at our expense. If we needed anything from him, it came at our expense. My dad made me feel that anything he did for me was such a big deal. What I have come to realize today is that what little my dad gave to me was nothing more than crumbs.*

Primary Vice

- *My dad was an escape artist. He would take his paycheck and spend most of it gambling. Then when it was time for him to come home, he would throw stones at my upstairs bedroom window to wake me up. I would have to sneak downstairs to let him in. In the morning, he would get up and make breakfast for everyone. He would be singing and be in a real playful mood. I knew he was just covering up for what he did. He would hang around until my mom would ask for money to pay the bill collectors. Then he was off. He wouldn't come home at all some nights. When we got evicted from the apartment because the rent didn't get paid, he blamed my mom for not keeping the bills in order. I knew it wasn't her fault. He had a way of making us feel that the family problems were our fault. He taught me to lie, to cheat, to deceive, and not to respect anyone else's feelings. When it came down to whose fault it was because something happened, he taught me to always blame some-one else as fast as I could. My dad taught me how to be a voodoo witch doctor and to cast the right spell on someone and to make him the fall guy for my mistakes.*

The miserliness of the magician father fills his self-serving stance in life. If he is in a tight spot, he blames, projects, and scapegoats the first person he can find. His ability to rewrite reality and to exaggerate situations to benefit himself makes him untrustworthy. Unfortunately the magician father preys on his son's need for fathering. He appears and disappears at whim. He is unable to take personal responsibility. The magician father borrows his false sense of power from various sources. He creates situations that benefit him at the expense of others. He tries to imitate someone who is strong and confident while hiding behind his wife, his family, or his make-believe stories and experiences.

- ◆ *For years I would help my dad live the lie that he was hurt on the job and could not walk without being in pain. He filed a lawsuit with his company in which he claimed he slipped and fell and hurt his back. When the insurance investigator would come around, he would have me help him to the door so that he could limp with a little more exaggeration. He would groan and moan, and I would try not to laugh. As soon as the interview was over, he would throw aside his crutches and throw himself into his arm chair so he could spend the rest of his day gloating over his victory of decep-tion. This went on for years. While he was claiming his workmen's compensation, social security, and disability checks, I would hear how stupid the government was; how ignorant his boss was; how the whole damn country was falling apart and he had all the an-swers. As I got older, this picture of my father and what he had to say versus what he actually did just didn't fit. I lost my sense of humor about his charades. Today he is still claiming that his injuries have disabled him. He still claims that the government should take care of him. Sometimes he tries to place guilt on me and to shame me into helping him financially. When I do give in to his pressure, I feel like I just gave drugs to a drug addict. My*

dad stills has this magic over me. I want to show him my affection.
I don't want to be used by him. I still get the two confused.

Delusional Idea

The magician father assumes that someone else will make up for his lack of emotional investment and availability. He becomes consumed by his own personal interests. He sees his family and children as additional responsibilities and appendages. His time with the family seems burdensome unless he can somehow mix business with pleasure. The magician father doesn't allow himself to relax with his family.

The son of a magician father wonders who his father really is as a man, a father, and a male. Because of the absence of emotional engagement, the son of a magician father lives by assumptions about events in life. Unfortunately, this leaves the son with a tentative and provisional stance toward life, too. He never has the chance to feel secure and to experience his father's support and dependability.

In the movie *Hook* we see an example of a magician father and his son. Robin Williams plays the role of a middle-aged lawyer, Peter Banning, who was once the legendary Peter Pan. Unfortunately, Peter has forgotten his past experiences of being a carefree and mystical boy who taught unwanted children in Neverland how to enjoy their life of imagination, friendship, and magic. Peter has forgotten the importance of friendship and storytelling. He is too preoccupied with his work and personal responsibilities. His son Jack sees his father as one who makes promises, but who doesn't carry them through.

One sad scene shows Peter trying to leave his busy office so that he can be on time for his son's last baseball game of the Santa series. Because of his preoccupation with his work, Peter sends an employee to go ahead of him and videotape what he will miss of his son's year-end game. Peter himself arrives after the game is finished. On the way to England to visit Granny Wendy, Peter tries to be reconciled with his son. He promises that he will go next season to six of his son's games. Peter uses his favorite promise, "My word is my bond." In retaliation,

Jack says sarcastically to his father, "Yeah! Junk bonds!" The expression on Jack's face clearly communicates that his father has offered him another false promise.

Peter's typical magician behavior continues when they arrive at Granny Wendy's. She greets Peter by saying, "Welcome home, boy." After Granny Wendy greets each of the newly arrived family members, she announces one house rule that everybody must obey. "No growing up. Stop, this very instant." When Granny Wendy hears what Peter does for a living, she claims that he has become a "pirate." While the children are having fun chasing one another and playing games, they come running into the bedroom of their parents. As usual, Peter is doing business over the phone and explodes at his children for making so much noise. In a flurry of anxiety and irritation, he has his wife remove the children from the room. Peter has forgotten what it is like to be a child, and it is only by recapturing what he has forgotten that Peter will be able to win back his son.

As the movie unfolds we come to see how a magician father is redeemed. Peter is forced to redefine his personal values and come into a new identity. In doing so, he must learn how to value happy memories and to rediscover the powers of imagination, laughter, play, and magic. Like Peter Banning, the magician father can rediscover his inner truth and become a loving and adventurous father. He only needs to realign his life with love for another. The magician father must show his willingness to fight for and defend his son. He needs to sacrifice and to demonstrate his love for his son. His son needs tangible evidence of a dependable love between them.

Relational Style

The man under the power of the Manipulator [Magician] not only hurts others with his cynical detachment from the world of human values and his subliminal technologies of manipulation, he also hurts himself. This is the man who thinks too much, who stands back from his life and never lives it. He is caught in a web of pros and cons about his decisions and lost in a labyrinth of reflective meandering from which he cannot extricate himself. He is afraid to live, to "leap into battle." He can only sit on his rock and think. The years pass. He wonders where the time has gone. And he ends by regretting a life of sterility. He is a voyeur, an armchair adventurer. In the world of academia, he is a hairsplitter. In his fear of making the wrong decision, he makes none. In his fear of living, he also cannot participate in the joy and pleasure that other people experience in their lived lives. If he is withholding from others, and not sharing what he knows, he eventually feels isolated and lonely. To the extent that he has hurt others with his knowledge and his technology — in whatever field and in whatever way — by cutting himself off from living relatedness with other human beings, he has cut off his own soul. Whenever we are detached, unrelated, and withholding when what we know could help others, whenever we use our knowledge as a weapon to belittle and control others or to bolster our status or wealth at other's expense, we are identified with the Shadow Magician as Manipulator. We are doing black magic, damaging ourselves as well as those who could benefit from our wisdom.[1]

- *I can still hear him shouting at us kids, "If you don't keep quiet in the house you'll drive me out again." The emphasis is on "again." My mom and dad fought a lot. She would cry, he would walk. I mean, walk out on the family. Then he would hold it over our heads any time he tried to discipline us. The threat of walking out became a warning anytime he wanted to get his way. My mom learned to jump at his every whim. I guess I believed in him when I was younger. During my high school years, however, I would look for ways to get his goat. Then, when he would threaten to leave us because of my behavior, I would ask him if I could help him pack his bags. Everything my dad did was tentative and provisional. If we did what he wanted, it was a peaceful home. If not, his demonic ways kicked in. There was only one way in this house and it was his way. He would do anything to make sure he got his way and at any price.*

- *I went on a retreat one weekend and the theme was "Healing of Memories." The retreat director led us into some imagery that was supposed to provoke unreconciled memories in our lives. One of the morning sessions we spent on remembering our fathers. Some people had to forgive their fathers for being too mean, or for not showing enough support or affection. Others shared moments of gratitude for what their dads had sacrificed for them. As the various accounts went on, I was lost! I had no memories! I realized that I had spent most of my childhood living off the dreams of what could be, what should be, or what I wanted my dad to be. I had no real memories of me and my dad. I had memories of me wanting my dad. I can remember watching TV and wondering if what I saw on some of the family shows could actually be true. I didn't need to heal memories. I needed to make some. I was devoid of memories of my dad. I came to realize that the big empty space in my chest was aching for some fathering.*

Dominant Fathering Qualities

He wants the power and status that traditionally come to the man who is a magician, at least in the socially sanctioned fields. But he doesn't want to take the responsibilities that belong to a true magician. He does not want to share and to teach. He does not want the task of helping others in the careful, step-by-step way that is a necessary part of every initiation. He does not want to be a steward of sacred space. He doesn't want to know himself, and he certainly doesn't want to make the great effort necessary to become skilled at containing and channeling power in constructive ways. He wants to learn just enough to derail those who are making worthwhile efforts.[2]

◆ *I remember one of the most humiliating days of my life. I was going to present my music recital for my master's degree in music. My mom had always been a real support to me. My dad? Well, I learned early in my life to downsize any successes I had when dealing with him. It was an unspoken rule in our house that you didn't ask for attention for what you accomplished. One, you would never get it from my dad, and, two, he was never there for me emotionally anyway. So it didn't matter what he had to say. I never felt his support while I was in school. Anyway, I was just about to begin my recital when my parents walked in late and had to be seated.*

I could hear his big mouth complaining that his seat was too far from the stage. He began to make a scene and stirred up all kinds of commotion. After everyone had noticed his hysterical behavior, he left.

At first I wanted to track him down and kill him. Then, I was concerned about what everyone in the auditorium was thinking. Should I apologize? Should I just act as if nothing happened? Well, I made it through my recital that night. When I got home, there he was sitting in his chair, greeting us all with a big smile. I knew it wasn't worth discussing his behavior. So we all acted as if nothing happened. My dad had us all incapacitated with his magical potion of silence and avoidance. I have a lot of things I would like to say to him about what I think and feel. But it wouldn't make any difference because the best I would get from him would be a cold shoulder.

Chapter 5

THE VILLAIN FATHER

————— ✑ —————

When I became a father I was overwhelmed with sadness. I knew that
I had to protect my child from something terrible.
                                    —Mike Lew, *Victims No Longer*

+ *I spent my whole childhood in fear of my dad's anger. He would
  emotionally blackmail us. He would pit us against my mom. Even
  if we did cooperate with him, we would still end up suffering
  some loss.*

+ *I watched him beat my older brothers and sisters. He would laugh
  afterward and claim we were weak. I wouldn't cry when he beat
  me, and I knew that drove him crazy. My sisters and brothers
  would beg him to stop beating me with the belt. The harder he hit
  me, the more defiant I became. I would never let my dad see me as
  a weak person.*

+ *Psychological torture would best describe how my father raised me.
  He was a bully. He would do his best to shame me, and if that
  didn't work, he would resort to physical abuse. I would get his
  permission to do something, and just when I was about to begin,
  he would come in and tell me that he never said I could do it. The
  only parental authority he had was his fist and a whip.*

+ *I lived on a farm and would do my best to hide from my dad. When
  he and my mom would fight, I knew it was only a matter of time
  and he would be after me. If he couldn't find me, he would go into*

the barn and begin to torture one of the farm animals. I could hear him yelling and screaming and beating on one of the cows. I was sad for the cow, but relieved that it wasn't me.

- *My dad would tease me. He would get me so confused I never knew what to believe. He always played these mind games with me. Just when I thought it was safe to let him into my space, he would take advantage of me again. Even today, I'm not sure what he wanted from me. Why was he so dishonest and such a liar?*

Primary Expressions

The villain father can be a bully, a perpetrator, a rage-aholic, and is often physically, emotionally, and sexually abusive. He has little control over his impulsive desires and reacts harshly toward his son. The villain father uses violence to contain and to control his son. Through the misuse of his parental authority, this type of father has no sense of proportion in his application of discipline and structure.

The villain father maintains his position as head of the household through the use of blame, shame, and covert and overt abuse. He provokes and intimidates his son so that the young man cannot usurp his father's authority. The father's manipulation and deception maintain a violent tension between father and son. Feeding the fires of anger and fear, the villain father traps his son in an atmosphere of love-hate. The son of a villain father struggles with hatred toward his father and yet longs to find some semblance of love and affection from his father.

- *I so much wanted my father to love me. In his quieter moments, we could work together on his car. I would be at his beck and call. I really enjoyed helping him. But at any moment, the smallest thing could set him off. I knew sometimes that it was something or someone else who made him get angry. Yet I was the closest person for him to dump on. He would curse at me and start pushing me around. If I cried, that would make him even more angry. I learned early on just to let him take it out on me so he could get over his anger. I wanted to help my dad. I always wanted to love him. Still, I always feared his temper.*

- *He would tell me how he was ready to kill anyone who would cross him. He said these things especially when he would be cleaning his hunting guns. Sometimes I would think that he was including me with those people he would kill. I wanted to be with my dad and hunt with him. But his stories of fighting and beating up people scared me. I think he wanted me to admire him for his power. Even when he would talk to strangers, he would talk with such arrogance. I wanted to find some good in my father. The older I got, the less able I was to see anything good in him.*

The villain father sustains a false sense of strength and power. For the sake of his own ego and gain, he trespasses and violates the personal boundaries of others' privacy. The villain father, like a raging adolescent without any awareness of consequences, strikes out at others in order to wound them and to gain authority over them. Any strength or autonomy demonstrated by his son becomes another opportunity for the villain father to conquer and to compete.

- *I was really good at football. I did a lot of weight-lifting and body-building throughout my high school years. I built a small gym in our basement and would have my friends over to work out. My mom and dad were separated, and I saw my dad only once a month at the most.*

  One day, when I was a senior in high school, my dad came by to visit. My friends and I were working hard because of an upcoming big game. My dad always seemed to have a chip on his shoulder. He was a big man himself. I guess that's where I got my large build. As my friends and I worked out, he started to tell the guys what they were doing wrong. I could sense the tension building in the room. I tried to lighten things up by asking my dad to come and help me. He just couldn't let go of nagging the other guys.

  Finally, my best friend snapped at my dad and told him to get off his back. I could see my dad smile as though he had won the war. He couldn't leave it alone. Now that my friend had shown his weakness, my dad went after it like a hungry hound dog. I

*could tell what was going to happen. I tried like hell to get my
friends to take a break and go outside. At first my friend snapped
at me and said, "Tell that asshole to get out of here." After a little
encouraging, my friend did take a break.*

*Then the worst happened. My dad followed him outside. I only
noticed his absence after we began to hear my dad and my friend
yelling at each other. By the time we climbed out of the basement,
my best friend was in my dad's face. I tried to get between them.
Then someone threw the first punch. Within seconds the rest of
the guys were on top of my dad, beating the shit out of him. I
was really torn up inside. That was my dad they were beating up!
Yet, I thought, he had no right to rag on my friends, especially on
my best friend. Finally, I got them to stop and my dad left with
a bloody face and a bad limp. I froze as I watched him leave. I
hated him for what he did, and I hurt for my best friend. But I also
hurt for my dad. He didn't come around for a long time after this
incident.*

Personal Fear

The villain father himself was once victimized. If he does not
resolve his conflicts or heal his wounds of the past, he will re-
create them in the life of his son. Unable to detach himself from
the trauma of his past, the villain father passes on to his son
what he believes are his rights and responsibilities. Traumas
and wounds from the father are passed on to the next generation. The villain father keeps his son blind to life-giving and
healthy choices by teaching his son that he is powerless and by
refusing to allow him to make his own decisions. We see in
this fathering style the "blind leading the (almost) blind."

The absence of any self-disclosure on the part of the villain father creates the inbreeding of pity, fear of loss, and a
defensive posture toward life and relationships. If the villain
father feels empowered, he can and will provide some semblance of leadership for his son. However, with any faltering
of his inflated ego, the villain father feels justified in being
compensated at the expense of others. He teaches his son how
to live off other people's strengths. He does this by victimiz-

ing others. This type of fathering sends a son into the endless peril of the victim-victimizer cycle. The villain father creates a negative reality out of the saying, "Like father, like son."

+ *My father taught me that you never turn your back because some-one will slip a knife in it. Trust no one and do your best to find something bad about others so you can use it to your advantage. The only way you maintain being first and the best is to make your competitor less than yourself. Find their weakness and exploit it. My father showed me how to do this by practicing these same skills on me. After he would trip me up and make me feel stupid, he would point out how this lesson would help me with my future as a businessman like himself. He taught me how to lie, cheat, de-ceive, and rip off people. He would take great pride in his ability to break another person and to gloat over his victory. My father would sell anything and anyone in order to get what he wanted. His insatiable appetite for power and success made everything he touched and everyone he met second-best.*

Trying to remain in first place and in a position of power is a primary drive of the villain father. He traps, oppresses, and exploits others for the sake of his personal pleasure and his quest for power. He victimizes his son in order to revisit his own sad experiences of life. Unable to share with his son, the villain father maintains both a physical and emotional distance from him. Any exchange between them usually comes at the expense of the son.

+ *I worked really hard as a newspaper delivery boy. I was in the seventh grade when I landed this job. Every morning at 5:00 a.m. I was up and off to deliver papers. The cold windy morn-ings were the hardest. But my mom would get up with me and cook me breakfast and give me a thermos of hot chocolate to take along. I had earned enough money to buy myself a new bike. I thought that with a better and bigger bike, I could carry more pa-pers and increase my paper route. I was so proud of what I had accomplished.*

When I got my last paycheck that gave me enough money to buy my bike, my dad took my money away. He took it all. He said that it was time that I began to pay him back for all the room and board he had provided me over the past years. I tried to argue with him that if I could buy the bike I could earn more money even faster. He said that he had to hand over his paycheck to his father and that it was time that I became a man and did the same thing.

I spent days trying to believe that what my dad did was right. After a time, I lost interest in working the newspaper route. I got fired because of tardiness. After that, I got into a lot of trouble. I started to hang out with kids who didn't like to go to school. When my mom and dad were called to meet with my teacher, my dad said that it was up to me to decide if I wanted to go to school anymore. He quit school when he was in the eighth grade and he, according to him, turned out just fine. He was a hardworking man and I could become just like him. Unfortunately, I did become just like him. I did quit school and ended up moving from one cheap job to another. I got into trouble with the law a couple of times, especially because of drinking and driving. When I look back at how my life turned out, I became my father. He helped me to repeat his life and his life choices. I wished I had someone else who could have turned me in another direction.

Primary Vice

Wounded from his past and unable to find relief from his own memories and lived experiences, the villain father is driven by a desire for revenge. He is haunted by memories of the past that influence and eventually determine his decisions and choices. Acting on impulse and maintaining a defensive posture toward life, the villain father has a warped sense of morality and a self-serving ethic. His own personal boundaries seem invincible and impenetrable. He moves between two extremes of being fearful and intimidated and behaving forcefully and fearlessly. Because of an unconscious desire to find some relief or reconciliation, he acts out traumas of the past with his son as a pawn. Unfortunately, revenge breeds revenge. The inability of the villain father to acknowledge his wounds and to dwell in the consciousness of his pain long enough to seek healing prohibits any resolution or reconciliation with his past.

All who are part of his social system are used for his unconscious acting out of anger and revenge. His circle of friends and associates is kept as long as they serve a purpose to help him revisit, re-create, and repeat unresolved traumas of the past.

- *I watched my father grow in his rage and anger. He would always apologize after beating me with a belt. He would say that a good father would only use his hand. While he would hit me, he reminded me that his father hit him and that it was meant to keep me honest and good. When he would yell at me, he would again remind me that his father did the same to keep him honest and good. When I was grounded or punished for breaking something in the house, again, he would compare my punishment with what his dad had done to him. I grew to hate my grandpa as much as I hated my dad. I felt as though every damn thing that my dad had to go through with his father had to be done to me.*

- *He would pout and whine over the smallest things that happened to him at work. He would come home and start to pick on any one of us kids. It was as though he were looking for something to bitch about. My mom ran around the house like a chicken with her head cut off. She and all of us tried to keep him peaceful and content. But it was to no avail. He would find something to complain about. Then he would begin to talk about how his father demanded so much of him. He would talk about how he had to manage the whole farm, go to school, and keep up with his studies all by himself. Then we would hear about how mean and cruel his father was to him and his mom. He complained that he had to do all of his father's work because his father was a no-good lazy son-of-a-bitch. I guess my dad didn't learn anything good from his father. We all had to live our lives in reparation for my grandpa's sins. I wished my dad could have learned to forgive his dad so that we could have had a life of our own.*

Delusional Idea

Why does a villain father believe that he has the right to hurt others and ignore the effects that such behavior has on his son or the family? The villain father believes, with his own twisted logic, that he is justified. He lives in an insulated world defined by his own attitudes and measured by his own values. If the son of a villain father adopts his father's way of thinking, believing, and behaving, he will become the next villain father. If the son tries to live and work within his father's isolated world, he will do so only by sacrificing his own values and personal self-worth. The son of a villain father either adopts his father's attitudes and behaviors or the son becomes the enemy of his own father.

This dramatic equation of father-villain and enemy-son can be seen in the movie trilogy *Star Wars*, which captures a variety of fathering styles mentioned in this book. Briefly, we can imagine Darth Vader as the villain father. Luke Skywalker, Darth Vader's lost and recently discovered son, is a good example of the champion father (see chapter 8). However, for Luke to attain his champion father position and destiny, he must be mentored by Old Ben, alias Obi-wan-Kenobi, a Jedi knight. In turn, Old Ben had to have been fathered, mentored, and championed by Yoda, the Jedi master, who is both mystic and champion father. Obi-wan-Kenobi admits that once he had tried to mentor Darth Vader. Tragically, Darth Vader turned from the good side of the force to the dark side of the force.

Darth Vader attempts to turn his son toward the dark force. He encourages his son, Luke, to join him in his efforts to gain ultimate power and control over the universe. As Darth tries to convince his son to be like him, Luke recalls his other, "second-chance" fathers, Ben and Yoda. He remembers his friends, Hans Solo (trickster become companion), Chewbacca, and Princess Leia, who have helped him to reach this point in his life. Luke's mission to champion the cause of the rebel alliance pulls deeply and strongly within him. By remembering the good side of the force, Luke is able to detach himself from his father's enticements to join him for control. Darth Vader finally declares that if his son will not join him then Darth must kill him.

The villain father shows little remorse for his lost son and family. Based on delusional thinking, he believes that his causes and goals are more valuable than those of the other family members. Always declaring his actions as justified, the villain father sacrifices anyone's health and well-being for his own personal objectives.

Relational Style

When left alone, the villain father protects himself with an armor of withdrawal and preoccupation. Whenever he engages in activities outside his own ego boundaries, he takes a defensive stance toward others. His gruffness is an attempt to scare off people. Yet he wants attention from others, especially from those who are significant to him. He exploits the weaknesses of those close to him. His passive-aggressive behavior is antisocial and inappropriate, particularly in social situations.

The villain father takes a passive-aggressive stance toward his son. He remains emotionally detached and indifferent when he is in his passive stage. During his calmer moments, the villain father provides his son with a tentative but safe environment. In order to fill the void created by his villain father's emotional vacuum, the son resorts to imagination, wishful thinking, and fantasies.

The son may identify with his father's aggression to gain his father's approval. He may attempt to ally himself with his father's ways of thinking, feeling, and behaving. On the other hand, for protection the son of a villain father may withdraw from his father, hoping that his father will calm down.

Some men who have survived living with their villain father have been able to use their inner resources to determine for themselves what is good or bad behavior. This inner judgment helps them to separate their father's bad and inappropriate behaviors from this wounded person whom they call "Dad."

However, the aggressive nature of the villain father feeds his delusional thinking. He believes that if he is to remain in control, he must be prepared to defend himself and to justify his behavior at any time. If the son buys into this same delusional thinking, the son will sacrifice much of his personal identity, self-worth, and even his sanity. Unless there are other victims who demand less energy, the villain father will consume much of his son's physical, spiritual, and psychological well-being.

• *When my dad was in one of his calm moods, I would dream about what it would be like to sit next to him. I mean really sit next to him. I wanted to touch him. I wanted to know what it would be like to feel his strength and to believe he would protect me. I would dream many times of being in life-and-death situations and my father would come to my rescue. I would dream of him crying with me when I almost died and that he saved me. I would dream of my dad holding me and telling me that he would be proud of me. Instead, my dad would notice periodically that I was staring at him. He would glare at me and ask, "What the hell is wrong with you? Why are you staring at me?" He couldn't see that I was looking at him with admiration and love. He would push me away again and again and again.*

• *I liked to go to church with my mom and sisters. When we would get home, however, my dad would be there waiting to start a torture session. First, he would complain about the church and how it had us all fooled. Then he would start on the minister and how he was out to get all our money. According to my dad, we were just too stupid to see that. Then I would get the special treatment. I would be called "faggot" or "queer" because I went to church. That was just for weak-minded men. If I had any balls, so said my dad, I would wake up and see that nothing good could come from going to church.*

• *I got to hang out with my dad and his friends at a local bar. I was about nine years old when I realized that my dad was a bigot. He and his friends would rag on just about everybody. First the "blacks," then the "spics," then the military guys, then women, and then the gays. I learned how to put people down and to talk just like my dad.*
  One day another father and son came into the bar. They might have been Hispanic. The man's boy was about my age. I went over and asked him if he would like to play pool with me. We began to have a good time. Then my dad noticed that my new friend was Hispanic. My dad pushed the boy away from the pool table

*and the boy fell to the ground, real hard. His father saw what hap-
pened and came running over to pick up his son. My dad and his
friends encircled the two of them. They began to push them both. I
was scared. The man begged them not to hurt his son. Then they
started to hit the man. I started to cry out and to beg my dad to
stop. My father came over to me and hit me hard across the face.
He said, "No spic-loving brat is going to tell me what to do." I
don't remember much after that. I do remember that my dad left
the bar without me. I grew to hate him and his friends. They were
cruel and mean to anyone who didn't fit their expectations.*

Dominant Fathering Qualities

At his best, the villain father may be stern, harsh, crass, stoic,
pushy, belligerent, or demanding. He presents himself as one
who is invincible and independent. Contrary to these appear-
ances, however, he carries himself as though he were burdened
and heavy-laden with life. His voice projects both sarcasm and
criticism. Many sons raised by a villain father perceived their
dads as almost never talking to them, and when they did, their
fathers yelled or spoke with unnecessarily loud voices. Even
the son of a villain father attempts to interpret his father's behaviors with some positive motivation; by so doing, he may
lessen some of the perceived violence. This stance may bring
about some temporary relief from the physical and emotional
constrictions that the son experiences. The father's persistent
need for control and power exhausts any possibility for his
son's trust and respect. The son must learn how to deal with
his father's thirst for control and power or he may become
intoxicated with the same addiction.

◆ *You've heard of the "loud" family? Well, I would like to intro-
duce you to the "scream" family. We always had to speak loudly
to get attention. I know where we learned this. My dad was a
screamer. Even when he was calm, he would bellow when he talked.
My mom always asked him if his hearing was impaired. Everyone
around the neighborhood could hear him. I felt that my dad talked
this loudly because no one really cared what he had to say. Once
my brothers and sisters were old enough to defend themselves,*

they would yell back at my dad. We never really talked with one another — we shouted. My dad taught us well.

- *My dad liked to break things to emphasize what he had to say. My mom would actually go and buy small breakable objects and leave them in the dining room so that he would have something to throw against the wall. I guess it was better for him to throw a plate or a plant against the wall than to throw one of his kids. When my dad wanted our attention, I would watch him build up to the moment when he would throw something against the wall. Then he would look to see if we all looked shocked. When I finally got to my teenage years, I learned how to fake looking shocked and scared.*

The villain father acts out aggressions with a vengeance. He places himself above the law both in the home and in the community at large. It is typical for this fathering style to demand that the children "pray, pay, and obey" while the father is a living contradiction of his demands. The villain father confuses his son about the virtues of loyalty, honesty, and commitment. He teaches his son one definition while he lives according to another.

- *My father would watch pornographic videos in the basement with his friends. I would watch them too sometimes. They would talk about how women really wanted to have "it" (sex). Then they would start talking about their own sexual activities. Sometimes they would describe to one another how they did it to so-and-so and how she wanted it so bad. I used to feel real bad after those experiences. Somehow it felt dirty and bad. Sometimes I would want to leave because I would start to feel sick. My dad would make me stay so that I could grow up and "be a man" just like him.*

- *I wasn't allowed in the basement when my older brother and dad were down there. I was about twelve years old, maybe thirteen, when I made the mistake of walking in on my dad and brother. They were having sex. My father was having anal intercourse with my older brother. They saw me, and that's the day it all began for me. I became part of their abuse. I don't remember much of the details, even today. I do remember crying a lot when I was in bed at night. My older brother would tell me that I would get used to it.*

He would assure me that he and I were special to dad because of what we could do with him in the basement. When I turned sixteen, I ran away from home. I got caught and was brought back home. When the social worker asked me why I ran away from home, I remember vomiting and curling over with cramps. I was rushed to the hospital. I never saw my dad again. He was put in jail. My older brother tried to get me to come to the basement with him, but I was big enough to fight him off. My older brother hates me because I got Dad put in jail. I still have nightmares about what my dad did to me and my brother. I still can't go into a basement without breaking into a heavy sweat.

The parent with this fathering style does not believe he has to justify his behavior, especially his parenting disciplines. Contradiction, moral imperatives, deception, threats, manipulation are but a few of the strategies used by the villain father. Confusing the differences between discipline and abuse, the villain father uses them interchangeably, especially when he is angry or wants to be in control.

• *When my mom and dad would fight I would stand there crying and beg them to stop. When my dad finished beating up my mom, he would start on me. I used to think that it was better for him to hit me than to hit my mom. Later, when I got bigger, I started to hit back. That made things worse. One day, mom and dad were at it again. I got a shovel from the garage. I began to hit my dad as hard as I could. He fell to the ground, but I couldn't stop hitting him. My mom tried to stop me. I wanted to kill him. He ended up in the hospital and never came home. I kept the shovel by the front door for years, just in case I had to use it again.*

• *As a businessman, my father had two sets of rules. The house rules and his business rules. The house rules were absolutes. There was no discussion and he always had the last word. I can see today that some of what my dad taught me has helped me as an adult. But his military dictatorship in the home made me fear him. I learned to cooperate, but with hatred. His fathering did not breed any love or affection. He was a tyrant and unmerciful. He beat me; he did not discipline me. I would go for days with bruises and whip burns and did my best to hide them at school. I always felt like I was just another "job" for him. Any inconvenience to my dad meant some kind of punishment for me. My dad's business was very successful. Everyone thought of him as a good businessman and a good Christian. He was well known in the community and served on various boards and city commissions. No one knew his dark side. That's the side that I had to live with.*

Domestic violence becomes the "playground" for some villain fathers. They maintain an illusion of control when they can cause disruption, confusion, chaos. This fathering style generates sadistic overtures that compel these men to strike out at others, especially their sons. For the sake of some personal gain, the villain father exploits others and thus becomes bound to a vicious cycle of destroy or be destroyed.

Part Two

THE EMPOWERED MALE AS FATHER

Five Healthy Fathering Styles

FIVE HEALTHY FATHERING STYLES

	ELDER	COMPANION	CHAMPION	MYSTIC	MENTOR
Primary Expressions	Concern, Interest	Personal relationship, Intimacy	Enthusiasm, Support	Awe, Wonder	Empathy, Encouragement
Personal Values	Collective knowledge, Tradition	Friendship, Loyalty	Individual excellence	Cosmic awareness	Wisdom, Learned experience
Primary Virtue	Respect	Trust	Patience	Hospitality	Deference, Humility
Divine Idea	Divine Word	Divine Union	Divine Love	Divine Spirit	Divine Humility
Relational Style	Affiliation, Rituals, Customs, Storytelling	Bonding, Mutuality, Befriending	Teamwork, Connecting, Cheerleading	Sharing, Guiding, Telling parables	Self-Containment, Interdependence
Dominant Fathering Qualities	Teaching, Fidelity, Purpose, Knowledge, Authority, Tradition	Bonding, Relationship, Endurance, Dependability, Faithfulness, Belonging	Stamina, Endurance, Humor, Perseverance, Play, Coaching	Spirituality, Groundedness, Connection to God and nature, Openness to intention, Memories, Eccentricity, Commitment to the cause	Advisor, Openness to showing others, Confidence, Instructor, Consultant

H OW DID YOUR DAD LEARN TO FATHER? What influences help to determine your fathering style? You are the by-product of your father's style of fathering. Your dad's fathering style was the by-product of his father's style of fathering. How you learned to father was also influenced by your male siblings, your grandfathers, and other male relatives, as well as your male teachers, coaches, and friends.

Learning how to father begins with our own fathers. Our fathers were not perfect, nor did they have within themselves all that is needed for *our* personal growth, happiness, and well-being. But dads at their best offer us a glimpse of what it means to be healthy male human beings. They show that fathering is both a pleasure and a personal challenge. They not only give a father's love; they also encourage, in their own way, the means to reciprocate that love.

Chapter 6

THE ELDER FATHER

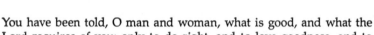

You have been told, O man and woman, what is good, and what the Lord requires of you: only to do right, and to love goodness, and to walk humbly with your God.

—Micah 6:8

♦ *My father was the rock of our church. He didn't just live our religious customs and traditions; he embodied them.*

♦ *We always addressed my dad as "Father" or "Sir" — not because he was removed from the family, but because his lifestyle encouraged respect and dignity.*

♦ *I remember my father on holidays. Those moments were very important to him. We all would come together to eat, celebrate, and enjoy the many stories he shared with us. My father became intimate during those family gatherings.*

♦ *My father was a great teacher and instructor about life and its meaning. He always had some lesson for me to learn and ponder. He made learning a special moment between us.*

♦ *Whenever I had a problem or concern, my father would refer to some lived experience he or some other family member had. He was great at remembering other people's lived experiences and graciously passed them on to me. I really appreciated my dad's belief in other people's goodness.*

Primary Expressions

The elder father is known by family and friends as a confident teacher and educator about life's experiences. He shows interest and concern for his son's ideas. His objectivity grants the space to allow his son to reveal, wonder, and question. Yet the elder father will not abandon his own point of reference, which includes those personal values and traditions that have proven reliable. The elder father relies upon the collective knowledge of his family, religion, and culture. Sometimes the details of his story may appear outdated, yet his beliefs and values are timeless. If we are willing to become the student, the elder father as teacher will appear.

The elder father may be perceived as aloof and distant. He takes an objective view of life to seek out its meaning and value. Because the elder father is intimately tied to the past, he approaches the future with caution and hesitancy. He is often slow to accept new ideas and, especially, new ways of doing things. However, once he is convinced of a new idea or procedure he becomes its ally and defender.

- *I remember coming home with great excitement about what I had learned in ecology class. I was a senior in high school, and I had just discovered how acid rain was infecting the trees in our area. I brought home my class notes and showed my dad. He and I began to read and study about this new phenomenon. I felt at times that my dad was so smart that there was nothing I could show him that he didn't already know. This was the first time in my life I can remember my dad watching and listening to me as I talked about my new discovery. He listened with such intense interest and wonder. We both began to collect articles about acid rain and its effects on our crops. Farming has been a long tradition in my family. My father was a great farmer. His devotion to the business of farming still resounds in my memory. Even more than that, however, I remember my dad's willingness to learn from me and to become an eager student. That taught me an invaluable lesson. No matter how smart you think you are, there is room for more learning and understanding.*

Personal Values

The elder father maintains trust in his values and beliefs. He is able to show respect, interest, and sincerity for differing ideas. He values his son's ability to think and take ownership of his choices and their consequences. The elder father will teach his son how to face a problem, to reconcile various solutions, and to seek out a resolution. He will do this from his lived and learned experiences. Helping his son to embody his values, especially those of the family traditions, is a primary value for the elder father. The elder father serves to remind his son of the family history and heritage. As his son moves toward independence from the family unit, the elder father encourages his son to maintain family routines, traditions, beliefs, and values.

- *When I got married, my dad took me for a long walk the day before my wedding. He and I talked a lot about family life, a good marriage, being a good parent, living honestly, keeping a job in perspective, keeping our religious faith and traditions alive while passing them on to the next generation, and what we each valued. My dad wasn't an emotional man. He and I walked real close to each other, and, once in a while, we would bump into the other and rub arms and elbows together. My dad stopped and looked me straight in the eyes and said, "Son, I want you to live your life with what you believe. That will carry you through the toughest moments of life. And when you need to be reminded of what you believe, drop by and I'll help you to remember." My dad died just a few weeks ago. I've been married for ten years, now. When I'm in those tough spots, I just remember walking down the road with my dad, and I ask him to help me to remember those values that I need to hold on to in order to get through this tough situation.*

The elder father embraces a way of life that expresses for him his inner beliefs and ideals. He sacrifices himself for the sake of those beliefs and ideals. His lifestyle, his home, his car, his clothing and ways of recreation reflect the personal beliefs of the elder father.

- *My dad was a minister in our small town church. He lived what he preached. Sometimes I'd wish he would preach a little less and* live a little more. But today I realize my dad could "talk the talk" because he had "walked the walk." He and I and my two other brothers were swimming one day in our neighborhood lake. I noticed that my dad would break loose from his usual composure when there were just the four of us present, but if someone from the neighborhood came by, he would cool it and take a low profile. I don't resent my dad for acting differently when others were around. I came to understand that he believed that he was to keep his private life private. Not many of my dad's congregation got to see him with his fun and playful side. But I did. Even now I feel honored that he shared this lighter side of himself with me and my brothers.

Primary Virtue

The elder father does not apologize for his authority or for the rules that guide his life. He is willing to share with his son what he believes in and what he values and why. He does not hesitate to share an understanding of his purpose and the meanings behind his behaviors and decisions. He typically invites others to mold their lives by what has guided him. He will help his son to sort out those traditions, rules, ethics, and boundaries that work best for him. Yet the elder father always defers to his son's own values and understandings to guide him.

* My father respected me. He taught me what respect is all about. He didn't demand respect. He invited it. I learned at an early age that respect is one of the most valuable attitudes to maintain. My dad taught me to respect the earth and care for it. He taught me to respect animals and to be good to them no matter what kind of animal it was. He taught me to respect people, regardless of color, creed, or gender. My dad's favorite one-liner was, "Every person, place, and situation is best treated with a little respect so that when it comes to your turn, that little investment of respect may have grown into a big return."

Divine Idea

The elder father is guided by the divine word. The fathering tools used by the elder father include calling his son by name, storytelling, providing insights, teaching, sharing wisdom and memories, helping, guiding, directing his son's responsibilities, putting a sense of order into situations, keeping harmony and duty in perspective, and giving his son's life purpose and meaning.

The elder father does not like to ramble, wander aimlessly, or waste time. He is known by his co-workers as hardworking and industrious. He usually keeps the same job for years. The elder father is considered by other workers to be fair, righteous, and dignified. His attitude of formality reflects care, graciousness, and integrity. He is an upright man, filled with the fear of the Lord.

The movie *The Chosen*, based on Chaim Potok's novel, portrays well the character of the elder father. There are four main characters. Reubin is a contemporary Jew; Danny Saunders, a Hasidic Jew. They live in New York City before and after World War II. The story itself is about these two young men as they study and attempt to understand their fathers. Danny's father is Rebbe Saunders, a heroic figure for his Jewish community. He is seen by his son as a righteous man who has many responsibilities. The father serves as a bridge between God and human beings. Danny says about his father, "My father saved his community [in Russia]. They would follow him anywhere. They consult with him about day-to-day matters, like what job should I get, who should marry my son or daughter or what to decide about this or that."

We can also see in this movie what happens when the elder father becomes caught up in his role as an authority figure. There is a scene where Reubin must be approved by Danny's father as an acceptable friend for Danny. At dinner one evening with the Saunders family, Reubin talks about his father's work and his hope that Israel will some day be a separate state. This idea is deeply offensive to Rebbe Saunders. He explodes with anger and a judgmental attitude. He declares that there is to be no more discussion about such a topic. Reubin's father, meanwhile, is becoming recognized both nationally as well as locally among Rebbe Saunders's followers. The rabbi quietly tells Danny that he cannot have anything more to do with Reubin. For Danny to disobey this directive would be to violate his father's beliefs and values. Reubin is confused about why such a separation should occur between him and his friend. Danny explains to Reubin that to violate his father's wishes would be horrible, something he could not do.

Another example of the elder father characterization can be seen in Rudyard Kipling's *The Jungle Book*. The elder father is Baloo, a big serious old brown bear who adopts Mowgli, a boy raised by the Seeonee wolf pack. Baloo is greatly respected by the wolf pack and all of the other animals of the jungle. He teaches Mowgli the law of the jungle and is known as the Teacher of the Law. Baloo's affection for Mowgli and his willingness to impart all that he knows about survival in the jungle — including his most precious secrets — speaks well of the wisdom of the elder father. Baloo wants to equip his son with all that he needs to live well and to survive the struggles of life that lie ahead.

Even wisdom can be abused, however. The elder father can become too dictatorial and narrow-minded toward the ideas of others, relying too much on his own opinions and values. The elder father can also become threatened if his ideas are not embraced with total dedication. If the elder father wants to remain healthy in his fathering, he must allow for diversity and open discussion regarding differing values and ideas.

Relational Style

The elder father affiliates with others through formal relationships, especially through ritual, custom, and conventional activities.

- *I remember Sunday afternoons. It was a dependable time. My dad would be waiting for me in the back yard with his horseshoes in hand. We would play for hours. Eventually, either the mosquitos drove us into the house or it became too dark to play. During those precious moments, my dad would begin to tell stories. He would remember his relatives and recall stories upon stories about these people. I would ask him questions about my school life, friendships, personal concerns, etc., and he would always share with me what had worked for him. My dad would give me options, not answers. He would sometimes answer a question with a question. He made me think. Somehow that kind of sharing bonded us together. I am so grateful that my dad loved me in this way. I became confident in my own abilities to sort things out. Today I feel very confident in my ability to process, introspect, and meditate on my life choices.*

When you interact with the elder father, you share emotions and feelings, but with subtle expression. The elder father will hurt with you when you fail and rejoice with you when you succeed.

◆ *I can still see my father at my college graduation. He stood there very tall, distinguished, and very proud of me. All during the ceremony, tears streamed down his face. He wouldn't lower his head for a moment as he looked at me with eyes of admiration and affection. After the ceremony, he walked up to me and hugged me with enough force to crush my ribs. I knew that in his clumsy and awkward way he was saying, "I am damn proud of you, son."*

The elder father may be perceived as out-of-date and at times simplistic in his ideas and understanding. He tends to wear conventional or conservative clothes. He is perceived as cautious, reserved, and sometimes aloof. Yet there is a quality of "presence" about him and a certain dignity in how he carries himself. He walks with pride and strength, and his very presence evokes respect.

◆ *My dad was a simple farmer. He had no formal education and could barely read and write. He spoke very little, but when he did his conversation was packed full of information and deep thought. One day there was a church meeting planned. A few angry parishioners wanted to get rid of the aging priest of the parish. I'm sure there were problems with the old priest, and he was no match for the rage and anger that had become so volatile with the parishioners.*

My father heard about this potentially explosive situation. On the day of the gathering, my dad put on his Sunday clothes, gathered us all together, and off we went to church. As we walked into church, I looked into my father's face and saw a look of authority and confidence. We all walked to the front of the church. My father looked out at all those who had gathered and said, "If Father Bryon is not welcome here at our church, I would like to invite him to my house to share his priesthood with me and my family. Anyone who would like to join us is more than welcome."

There was dead silence. It felt like hours passed before someone spoke up, "Sam, I'll be at your house this Sunday." Before you knew it, a majority of people had come forward and said the same thing, "Sam, I'll be at your house for Sunday church." Before we left the church my father said to the parishioners, "Seeing there are going to be so many guests at my house this Sunday, I guess I should ask Father Bryon if we could borrow the church?"

Dominant Fathering Qualities

When it is time to relax, the elder father generously shares his sense of fun and enthusiasm for play. He likes orderly activities that provide some structure and purpose.

- *My father would ask each of us children (all six of us) if we had finished our homework. That question was the cue to signal game time. If we had shown that all homework was complete, my father would let one of us pick a game in which everyone could share. I watched my father become transformed during those times. He would giggle, laugh, challenge, and tease us. My father would play with us as though he were just one of the children. Yet he would never lose his proper role as head of the household. When we finished the game, he would direct our clean-up activities and help wrap up the evening with preparations for the morning schedule.*

- *My dad taught me there is a time to play, a time to work, and a time to rest. I appreciate his sense of duty, honor, and order. When he was busy working at home and I wanted him to help me with something, he would make it clear that I was next on his list of priorities. I had to learn to wait my turn.*

- *I remember watching my dad going off to work to the nearby factory. As he walked to work, people would nod their heads and say "Good Morning" to him. I noticed that they didn't offer this gesture to others that they passed on the way to work. I realized only years later that my dad was considered by others to be a "spiritual" man. He was continually brought in to negotiate arguments and fights between the employers and union workers. He was considered a diplomat at the factory.*

- *My dad was always cautious and hesitant. Or so it appeared to me. Later in my life I realized that this was not the case at all. He was prudent and patient. My dad never pushed his ideas on me or led me to believe that what I wanted to do was less than important. He would wait and watch me struggle with my ideas. When I asked for help, he was there in a flash. I now realize that my father gave me the space to learn by myself until I was ready to ask for help. I now see what a wise man he was.*

The elder father will sacrifice his very self for his family. His dedication to protect and to provide for his family runs strong in his value system. He always maintains his identity as head of the household. Discipline, parenting, and household decisions are taken seriously by the elder father. He wants to know even the little details about family life. The elder father presides over family occasions. Holidays, birthdays, and special family gatherings are welcome times when the elder father shows his pride and affection for family members. He honors the elders of the family, especially grandparents. The elder father is deferential and humble in the midst of those who are older and more experienced than himself.

Chapter 7

THE COMPANION FATHER

My personal relationship to him was not as toward a father, but as toward an elder brother; and he, by his constant conversations with me and his extraordinary stories, greatly assisted the arising in me of poetic images and high ideals.
—G. I. Gurdjieff, *To Be A Man*

- *T.J., my dad's nickname, built a baseball diamond in the back yard. All the kids in the neighborhood would come to the back door and ask if my dad would come out and play with them.*

- *Everyone called my dad "Shorty," even though he was 6'6" tall. He had a way of knowing what I was feeling and thinking, even before I could put it into words. He was my first best friend. All my friends would say that they wanted my dad for their father.*

- *My dad would help me work out in the back yard before a baseball game. He would challenge me, encourage me, yell at me, laugh with me, and cry with me. He got as excited as I did about winning and just as sad about losing. He was my buddy and friend. He taught me a lot about caring. He did it so well.*

- *I was in a serious car accident. My dad never left my side those two weeks while I was in and out of consciousness. He cried with me. He made me laugh until I begged him to stop because it hurt to laugh. He bathed me, fed me, told me stories, and reassured me every time I wanted to quit and die. He understood all my lit-*

tle fears and put up with my terrible mood swings. He was my kindred spirit. Today, he is still my best friend.

♦ *I always thought of my dad as a companion, not really my father. He was always just one of the kids, one of the guys. We would take long walks and share our ideas, thoughts, questions, and concerns. He would ask me questions and I would ask him questions. We helped each other. He taught me what it meant to be a good listener and a faithful friend.*

Primary Expressions

The companion father has a natural gift for friendship. He can care for and befriend many people. His sense of humor and wit gives him the cutting edge to cope well with his son, especially during the teenage years.

The companion father is comfortable with intimacy, self-disclosure, and just hanging out with his son. It is typical for the companion father to work alongside his son. Working together, taking turns, sharing in the experience is of primary importance to the companion father.

♦ *I remember when I was eight years old, I wanted to build a fort. My dad said we could do it together. By the way, my dad is a research scientist and can be dangerous with a hammer and nail. I can remember us both lying on the ground with our initial blueprint of the tree fort. We worked all day long, sweating, laughing, teasing, and blaming the tree for all our mistakes. When the tree fort was complete, we both spent the first night together in our tree fort. We left a large hole in the ceiling so we could look at the stars. Later that evening, we had a major rain storm pass through. We had to abandon the fort due to flooding conditions! We still talk about that tree fort and argue over whose idea it was to make that big hole in the roof.*

Personal Values

♦ *My dad could help me understand human relationships. I would ask him all kinds of questions about girls, dating, sex, and why I kept getting into fights with Johnny Douglas. My dad always had some good ideas that spurred us into long conversations about life, its meaning and mysteries.*

The companion father values friendship. Making friends and keeping in touch with friends is very important to him. Like a good friend and faithful companion, the companion father works through the pain with his son. He wants to be a part of the memory-making. He puts himself into the lived experiences of his son. Making memories and taking time to explore with his son is also a personal value for the companion father. He shares in the good times and in the bad times. An important part of the companion father's relationship with his son is attending his son's sports and school activities.

The companion father has a way of offering hospitality to his local neighborhood. He is known for hosting and befriending other children of the neighborhood. His ability to be with and for others makes him a popular person. He is often remembered by others as friendly, kind, caring, available to help out in time of need, and ready to create community with lots of different people. One man remembers his dad as the prototype for Boy Scouts of America. "My dad had all the virtues of being an excellent Boy Scout."

Primary Virtue

Developing a mutual sense of trust and learning how to be with others is a special quality of the companion father. Trust is enhanced by learning how to respect each other's differences and by showing reverence toward others. An inseparable intimacy is created when father and son share mutual endeavors and learn how to depend upon one another.

- *I can remember my dad helping me learn how to ride a bike. My first day out on my brand new bike I was hit by a drunk driver. I spent months recovering. When I was well enough, my dad would walk alongside me, holding the bike and talking to me. As long as I heard his voice, I felt reassured. Then one day he told me he was going to get me going on the bike by walking along with me as*

I rode the bike, but then he would gradually let go. He promised that he would keep talking to me so that I knew he was still with me. I can still feel that moment when I realized he was no longer beside the bike. My dad was about ten feet behind me, still talking to me and reassuring me that I could handle this bike. Today, when I'm not sure of myself and insecure, I can still imagine my dad standing right behind me. I can hear him reassuring me and telling me, "Mike you can do it!"

Because the companion father has a trusting stance toward life, he has a receptive and proactive stance toward life events. He teaches his son how to discover the good in bad situations and to trust his own intuitions and abilities.

♦ *Any time I would ask my dad for his opinion, he would ask me, "What do you think is best for you to do?" As I considered my options, I would carefully look for his approval of at least one solution. Once in a while my dad would slip and show a bit more interest or enthusiasm for one idea over another. Most of the time, however, he would keep his opinions well hidden until I chose one. Then we would compare notes on his ideas and choices versus mine. My dad never asked me to do anything that he himself wasn't willing to do first. I learned at an early age to trust my hunches and believe in what I felt to be right for me.*

Divine Idea

The companion father has the ability to bond with his son and share in the empowering effect of mutuality. The willingness to share time, talents, and resources provides a coupling effect. The union between son and companion father provides the son with twice the strength and confidence. The union between father and son creates an intuitive belonging. The opportunity to know one another on a deeper level strengthens the relationship between them. The companion father is not limited to an exchange of words between himself and his son. The ability to communicate with subtle gestures, eye contact, intuitive hunches, and premonitions evolves throughout the relationship.

In the TV series *M*A*S*H*, the relationship between Hawkeye Pierce and his father well represents these qualities of
the companion father and his son. Hawkeye continually relies
upon his father's support, advice, and companionship. Hawkeye also refers to his father as his best friend, consultant,
advisor, helper, and listener. The letters they exchange are
letters between two best friends.

◆ *I served in Vietnam. My troops were responsible for transportation
of equipment. One really warm night, the sounds of the evening
kept most of us awake. It sounded like an echo chamber with frogs,
bugs, and birds screeching throughout the night. I had a picture
of me and my dad in my wallet. I would usually spend some time
thinking, praying, and remembering a day that my dad and I spent
at the beach. My dad would throw me into the water and we would
play all kinds of games. Suddenly, during these warm memories,
my troops were shelled. Equipment began to fly through the air.
All I can remember is the sound of a helicopter and a voice saying,
"You'll make it Scot. Hold on!" Then I vaguely remember waking
in a hospital barracks. I was in a lot of pain. My legs were numb. I
was told that I had been hit in the back with some mortar shells. It
was too early to tell if I would ever walk again. I tried not to cry.
Later that evening, the chaplain brought my wallet to me with my
dad's picture. The chaplain said that my dad looked like a fun kind
of guy. I fell asleep wishing my dad were with me. If only I could
hear him tell me one of his crazy stories or jokes.*

*When I fell asleep, I had this dream. My dad came walking into
the hospital. He was dressed like a clown. He began to tell me some
of his favorite jokes, and we laughed. He leaned over my bed and
said, "Son, I'm here with you. I hurt with you. I will not forget
you for a minute. You will walk again. Okay? Everything will be
all right. I love you, Scottie." I awoke from this dream and was
calling out for my dad. The night nurse asked me to get back into
bed. I was standing. I could feel my legs throb with pain. I was
standing. I would walk again.*

*My mom wrote me a letter recounting the following episode. It
was the same night that I was shelled and wounded that my dad
also had a dream. My mom said that dad jumped out of bed. He*

went to his trunk where he stored all of his costumes and put on his clown's mask. He walked to my old bedroom and was sitting on the bed. He was talking to the bed as if I were in it. He kept saying "Son, I'm with you. I hurt with you. I will not forget you for a minute. You will walk again. Okay? Everything will be all right. I love you, Scottie." My mom said that then my dad began to cry. She knew then that something had happened to me. Within a few days, they received a letter informing them that I had been hurt and hospitalized. Within two weeks I would be released and return to the States. It was not expected that I would walk again because of the massive damage to my spinal cord.

Before I got home, my dad had already contacted a neurologist, had moved my bedroom to the main floor of the house, and had built wheelchair ramps in the front and back entrances to the house. He went to the library and checked out every book that dealt with nerve damage, physical therapy, and trauma syndrome. He greeted me at the airport and ushered me into a program of intense rehabilitation.

Today I still have a slight limp. My dad lived out his promise. He never left my side until I could walk. Thanks, Dad, for hurting with me. It's true that "a burden shared is half divided."

The beginning stages of a father's moving into ownership of the companion fathering style are detailed in the movie *Ordinary People*. Conrad, a young teenager, struggles with the fact that he survived a boating accident in which his older brother, Buck, drowned. His mother, Beth, seems unable to show any affection for Conrad and pits herself between her husband and her son. Calvin, Conrad's father, reflects the conflict between absolute and undivided loyalty to his wife and her wants on the one hand and the desire to include his son in his love and affection on the other. Throughout the movie, we can see how Calvin tries to enter into his son's experiences, attempting to show interest and concern. Only after Calvin confronts his wife about her emotional unavailability to Conrad does Calvin begin to emerge as a redeemed companion father.

By the end of the movie, Calvin begins to make emotional

contact with his son by scolding him and showing his anger. Conrad interprets his father's anger as an emotional invest- ment in their relationship. He encourages his father to yell at him and to "ride his ass," like he used to for his dead brother. Calvin confesses that he never felt he had to watch out for Con- rad because his son was so hard on himself. The movie ends with father and son sitting on the back patio steps sharing their unspoken love for each other. This type of mutual shar- ing is typical of the companion father. He shares with his son as one who is his equal. He welcomes his son into his own deep thoughts and questions about life, love, and living. His son welcomes him in return.

Relational Style

The companion father bonds quickly. He lets it be known that he must feel like he belongs to something before he can make a personal investment in it. This quality of being connected will not take away from the relationship but will rather empower it. Belonging and being connected cements the relationship with assurances that no matter what the son does or becomes, the father companion will always be a part of him. The companion father will commit himself to this relationship and be available to his son whenever there is a need.

- *I had just been promoted to executive manager. My wife was hav- ing a difficult pregnancy. I wasn't coping well with all the changes of job, family, and marital life. I remember wanting to cry over the phone when my dad asked how my job and family life were going. I gave the "stiff upper lip" line and reassured him all was well. He must have read between the lines. That night, I came home and my wife greeted me at the door. She said there was a surprise in the living room. I walked in and there was my dad. When he hugged me, I caved in and cried. My wife joined us in the circle. We stood that way for a long time while my dad hugged both his son and daughter-in-law. That evening, we talked late into the night about what was really happening in my life. The next morning, before I got up for work, my dad had already left for home.*

◆ *I can remember that my mom, my sister, and I would go running with my dad. He would tease us along the way if we got tired. My dad's attempt to run to his expected goal usually got sidetracked by our horsing around. I always looked forward to that time with my dad. We would talk, run, reminisce, and imagine the future. Today, I run with my son and my wife. It is our special time together. My dad gave me a wonderful gift.*

Dominant Fathering Qualities

◆ *I always remember calling my dad by his first name. Strange, isn't it? I also remember my friends called my dad by his first name, too. My dad, Chet, was always ready to talk to any of my friends. He became the neighborhood counselor. By the way, my dad was a mechanic. Any time my car or the car of one of my friends broke down, my dad would bring the tools over to their house and help them work on the car. We always ended up with a group of my friends assembled by the time we finished fixing the car. Chet always knew what to ask you to get a good conversation going. My favorite story involving Chet is about the time some girls in my senior high school class were driving by my house one day. They were trying to see if me and the guys were hanging out together there. Their car broke down a few houses up the street. One of the girls came to the house and asked if I could help them out. I asked Chet if he could help. We all ended up working on the car. This is how I got to know the girl who would later become my wife. We still talk about that day when Chet brought us together.*

The companion father works side by side with his son. He provides the time and space in which to seek adventure with his son. The joy of this fathering style is found in working together and sharing experiences. The companion father has a way of creating excitement and enthusiasm for any job that he and his son share. The companion father is dependable, faithful, and approachable. His presence invites relationship. He expresses his feelings and emotions. He laughs and cries easily with his son. At times, he may be perceived as sensitive, sometimes too sensitive. He makes friends for a lifetime. He demonstrates his affections with hugs, kisses, hand-holding, closeness, and words of affection.

* *We would be walking down the street and my dad would kind of hang onto me. I never thought much of it. When we would be standing in line at a baseball game or movie theater, my dad would lean on me with his arm around my shoulders. His expressions of affection only became noticeable to me when I became aware that other guys' dads didn't do this. At first, I began to question my father's public display of affection. Then I came to realize that my dad shared his affection this way with all my friends. Sometimes I would become jealous if my friends got more attention from my dad then I thought I was receiving. They would hang on him, and my dad would always seem to be there for them. When my dad noticed that I was sulking or distancing myself from him, he would give me that cocky look that seemed to say I was still his son. He didn't need to get stingy because there was enough for everybody. Later in life, I realized that my dad was a loving friend to a lot of people. He always seemed to be at home with his body, masculinity, and self-image. I believe, today, that I can be myself with most people because my dad taught me how to be real.*

Chapter 8

THE CHAMPION FATHER

———————— ✆ ————————

Champion the right to be yourself; dare to be different and to set your own pattern; live your own life and follow your own star.
— *The Art of Living*

♦ *My father was a golf pro. Everyone in town knew him for his success. I wanted to play baseball. My father learned everything he could about baseball and taught me as much as I could learn. Today my professional career in baseball exists because of my father's encouragement. His interest in golf never interfered with my desire to learn another sport. I discovered my personal pathway in excellence because of my father.*

♦ *I couldn't walk as a child because of cerebral palsy. My father would create these outrageous obstacle courses for me to conquer. He believed in me. His hope for me to succeed would tap into my own desire to achieve, accomplish, and conquer. I learned to persevere and grow in strength because my dad believed in me. He was my cheerleader. Today I work with physically disabled children and I empower them, as my dad empowered me.*

♦ *Tennis was my love. My dad came to every game I played. I wasn't that good. Yet I had fun competing. Dad would write down my game's strengths and weaknesses. We would spend hours talking about how to improve my strategies. For my birthday I could always expect a new book on my favorite tennis pro. My dad never played tennis himself. He was a scientist. He championed me and let me become the most I could be. He was my number one fan.*

* *The elementary/high school that I attended didn't have much money or resources to help me with my learning disability. I remember hearing statements that I would not have to attend college. It was suggested that I plan on attending some trade school. My dad spent hours researching and learning about my disability. He helped set up a program that helped me to conquer my inability to read, memorize, and work with numbers. My dad never attended college. He helped me every day with his assurances that nothing is impossible. He would say, "If you believe in yourself, Tom, you can achieve anything." Today I am a college professor. I train future educators about believing in their students, just as my dad did for me.*

* *He never gave me an inch by which to slip. Everything I wanted I had to earn. I wanted to be like my dad, the physician. He would give me all the time, the energy and interest I needed when medical school studies became impossible for me. He encouraged me through those times when I wanted to quit. My dad never pushed me into any particular career. His favorite question was, "Bobby, what would make you happy?" Now I am a very happy physician. I have the greatest respect for my dad. He taught me by example how to be a supportive presence to my sons without getting in their way.*

Primary Expressions

The champion father shows affection for his son through enthusiasm, eagerness, and personal encouragement. He desires what is the best for his son and helps him to achieve just that. The champion father teaches his son how to accomplish, achieve, and excel as a unique individual. He sacrifices his own desires, plans, and designs for his son so that his son's dreams and desires can emerge. The champion father provides empowerment, challenge, and endurance to his son. He hopes that his son will become the best that he can become during the father's lifetime. Sharing in the successes and failures of his son become opportunities for the champion father to help his son seek the wisdom of the moment.

The champion father encourages his son to develop his own style, temperament, and attitudes. With loving perseverance, the champion father learns to enter his son's frame of reference as his son searches and matures toward adulthood.

- *My dad never asked me to do anything that he had not tried or wasn't willing to try. He and I would dare one another with new experiences. If either of us came up short, it never became a chance to dominate, but rather to affirm the differences. My mom would like to experiment with new international foods. I remember the first time I tried to eat Ethiopian food that my mom had made for us. My dad and I looked skeptical, so we assured one another that we would put a spoonful in our mouths at the same time. If we survived, we would reward ourselves with an extra portion of ice cream. We did survive. We celebrated the moment with lots of ice cream. My dad taught me that he wasn't above trying something new. Even today, I try to keep that attitude with me. Thanks, Dad.*

- *I needed to pass the exercise routines for our gym class in order to pass to the sixth grade. I was overweight and in bad physical condition. My dad built me a small gym in the garage. He would meet me every day after work. We would challenge one another to see who could do the most sit-ups, push-ups, and other exercises. It became a special moment for us. My dad would sometimes let me outdo him in one routine or another. He showed me that I had physical abilities that were only dormant within me. He never taunted me or put me down for being overweight. Today I am in excellent condition. I still have to watch my food intake because I can easily gain weight. My dad still works out with me at the local gym. We challenge one another, and sometimes I let him outdo me. I guess I owe him a few.*

Personal Values

Because the champion father has walked his own path of personal excellence, he can effortlessly help his son down the same road. This particular fathering style finds pleasure in his son's abilities no matter how they differ from his own. He can help his son achieve personal excellence too. Patient with his son's struggle to come into his own, the champion father does not take any shortcuts to assist his son in achieving his own destiny.

The champion father believes in sacrifice, stamina, endurance, tolerance, and discipline with a purpose. He teaches his son how to survive difficult moments, and he does not usurp his son's need to feel the pains of growth.

♦ *I can still see my dad's eyes as he watched me wipe out on the ice. I realized at the moment that I had lost the competition. After all those hours of training, all that money and time, I had failed. I thought about all the traveling with my dad and all his lost time from work and the money he had spent on me. I can remember distinctly saying to him as he greeted me on the ramp to the locker room, "I failed you, Dad." He looked at me and said, "Son, all I ever hoped for you is that you would do your best. I have no regrets for all that you and I did to get you to this point. How about you?" I struggled not to cry. He held me and said, "Even the great ones have to learn how to survive a fall like you took today. You and I will learn a great deal from this one. Don't you agree?" I can still see my dad's eyes. He wore for me a look of hope and belief in me that carries me through difficult times, even today.*

Primary Virtue

Patience is the primary virtue of the champion father. He has a capacity to wait without judgment. He is slow to draw conclusions, hoping not to shortchange what could be. With the quality of serenity the champion father possesses the ability to be with his son in difficult moments and to help him through his decision-making process. The champion father has a kind of spirit that has been tempered with the wisdom to know when to "lighten up" and take a break. He brings to his son a great sense of humor. A hallmark of this fathering style is the ability to make light of failures and yet to learn from them.

- *My dad's favorite question after I had made some blunder was, "What did you learn from your mistake, Randy?" He would not review what I did wrong. Instead, he would help me to look at what had gone wrong and to see how I could do it better the next time. Every blunder I made was an opportunity to learn. I never felt ashamed to admit my mistakes to my dad.*

- *My dad used to remind me that human beings are built to make mistakes. The differences between people were between those who learned from their mistakes and those who didn't. Those who didn't kept making the same mistakes throughout their lives.*

- *I think the serenity prayer speaks well of my dad. He would help me find the courage to change the things in my life that I could change. Those things that I couldn't change, he would help me to live with in peace and acceptance.*

Divine Idea

- *I watched my dad struggle with his own addictions to alcohol and cigarettes. After he had finished a thirty-day residential addiction treatment program, he had changed. I remember him talking to me about how he had never loved himself. He always felt that he was inadequate and inferior to others. What he learned from his newly found Twelve Step AA program was that he is okay just the way he is. He recently learned how to love himself, and he wanted me to know that he needed to share this newfound insight with me. I was twenty-eight years old when my dad began to teach me how to love myself. We were learning together how to undo the damage of shame and guilt. My dad would jokingly say to me, "I guess you're never too old to learn how to love yourself."*

The champion father has grown in a self-love that guides him. He taps into his own experience of self-worth and acceptance, which gives him the capacity to show this love to his son. Being at home with his own body, feelings, sexuality, and identity gives the champion father the stability to nurture his son into a personal identity and a healthy sexuality. Loving the differences between himself and his son creates a bond of unity between son and father. Learning from one another takes place because the champion father welcomes differences and distinctions between himself and his son. He takes pride in nurturing his son to become someone special.

Encouraging his son to make decisions based on personal values and self-love reflects well the virtue of the champion father. The champion father is guided in the care for his son's welfare by deciding what is best for himself and for his son's particular needs.

* *My dad had a zeal for sports. He played everything, and he did well in everything he did. I would say that my dad was a big kid who loved competition and a good workout. He would beam with joy when he had the chance to engage in some athletic activity. He and I were opposites. I liked to read a good book or go to the movies. I liked to experiment in our garage with chemicals and electrical gadgets. Once in a while my dad would persuade me to get involved in some sports activity. But his real love for me was shown when he would buy me a science magazine that had some new gadget I could order to use in an experiment.*

    I also realized that my dad was a true champion when I would be completely engrossed in some big experiment and he would quietly slip in to see how I was doing. He would quiz me and check out everything I did. He really was interested in my personal love for science and experiments. When some of my brothers or sisters would tease me for not being as athletic as my dad or themselves, my dad wouldn't stand for their criticisms. He assured them, and me, that each of us has a place in which to find our happiness. His was on some sports field, while mine was in the garage. Both were equally good by the fact that each of our choices made us happy. Today, I am a research scientist for a pharmaceutical company. My work allows me to do what I have always enjoyed doing, that is, research and experimentation. I frequently take my dad to various sport activities. I watch him become one of the most enthusiastic fans as you'll ever find. He is still a big kid when it comes to sports. And I love to be with him when he is.

The champion father walks a figurative tightrope when he begins to engage his son and encourages him to excel in his personal pathway to excellence. It would be tempting for the champion father to live out his unfulfilled dreams through his son's life. The champion father faces the danger of becoming zealous for his son's accomplishments. He can begin to nag and complain instead of offering encouragement and challenge. If the son of a champion father does not meet with his father's expectations, then undue pressure to please his dad can become a driving force for the son's desire to excel. This kind of situation can lead his son into feelings of compromise, resentment, and conditional acceptance. Then it could happen that the son of the champion father would live his life for his father's pleasure and approval. The son could easily lose his own personal sense of worth and integrity.

How the champion father satisfies his own need for excellence has a great influence on his ability to nurture and care for his son's needs. The champion father must have a healthy balance in his own life that embraces his personal expectations for self-achievement and accomplishment. Such a stance toward his own life is integral to the champion father's ability to love his son with unconditional love and acceptance.

In *The Karate Kid*, a novelization by B. B. Hiller based on the major motion picture of the same name, the champion and the competitor are well contrasted. Daniel LaRusso moves to California with his mother. He soon gets into conflict with Johnny and his gang, the Cobras. These young high school students are training with the *sensei*, the martial arts teacher named John Kreese.

> He was a dangerous looking man with cold, piercing eyes — the sort of person who just looked like he'd strike first and strike hard. He taught his students, "[You] . . . lose concentration in a fight and you're dead meat. We do not train to be merciful. Mercy is for the weak. Here, or on the street, or in competition, if a man confronts you, he is your enemy. An enemy deserves no mercy."

In contrast to John Kreese, there is Mr. Miyagi, who adopts Daniel as a student. He tries to teach Daniel that there is no such thing as a bad student, only a bad teacher. Mr. Miyagi tells

Daniel, "First step is sacred deal. I teach karate, that my part. You learn, that your part. I say. You do. No question. Deal?" An unusual training program for Daniel begins, which includes washing cars and painting fences and the house. Each assignment has a very specific way of using the hands and arms. Included in these vigorous exercise routines are instructions for proper breathing.

> Mr. Miyagi was holding a bucket of soapy water, a sponge, and several towels in his hands. Before [Daniel] knew what was happening, Mr. Miyagi unceremoniously slapped the soapy sponge into Daniel's extended hand. Then, he pointed to the cars in the yard and said, "Good. First wash. Then wax. Like this," making small clockwise circles with his right hand. "Wax on, right. Breathe in, breathe out." "Wax off, left," he said, making counter-clockwise circles with his left hand. "Breathe in, breathe out, very important, breathe in, breathe out."

Each assignment that Daniel was given had a greater purpose — his karate skill development. Mr. Miyagi taught Daniel by championing his skills and discipline.

The story called *The Champ* is an example of how a champion father may violate his son's trust when the father cannot maintain the integrity of his own skills and past successes. Billy is the has-been prize fighter who pours out all of his love on his eight-year-old son, T.J. Billy's wife, Annie, has left both him and his son for fame, money, and the glamorous life. T.J. is a strong and brave young son. At eight years of age he is uncritically adoring of his father — guardian of the scrapbooks, shameless aper of his father's mannerisms. T.J. imagines his father to know it all; he had been champion of the world and had arms like iron and an iron will to match. And there was nothing T.J. could see to suggest that the Champ was in anything less than his prime.

"His son was proud of him. But there were some things he didn't want his son to know. Because he didn't want his son to worry or be afraid. He wanted his son to be strong, and he was strong. He was proud of his son." However, Billy slowly slips out of his disciplined ways and begins to count on good luck. He starts to gamble and drink. He hides these weaknesses from T.J., who can only see discipline and responsibility in his father. T.J. believes his father is truly a courageous and disciplined champion.

Throughout this downward spiral, Billy allows his son the independence and the opportunities to strengthen himself through his own adventures. This attitude of freedom for his son is typical of the champion father. Unfortunately, the Champ tries to live his own life without a disciplined structure. He allows T.J. to assume the role of the adult in some situations. T.J. rises to the challenge. He covers up for his dad when he drinks too much or spends T.J.'s money without the boy's permission.

When the champion father tries to live a life based only on past accomplishments, he deludes himself.

Relational Style

The champion father holds a mystique for his son. Admiration, respect, and desire to emulate his father are typical of the son who has a champion father. A son can learn how to handle success, responsibility, social status, and power from observing these qualities in his champion father. If his father has been acknowledged as a professional, a hero, or a successful man, the son can glean from his father's personal secret keys to becoming successful as well.

The champion father is both co-worker and teacher to his son. He will work with his son, struggling and contributing to his son's success. Yet the champion father will not do the work for his son. He will share his personal stories and help his son learn from other resources. But it is the son who must make the application and do the hard work in order to achieve.

The champion father helps to provide his son with the time and space to accomplish some tasks on his own. This father will carefully safeguard the psychological space his son needs in order for the young man to explore his personal path toward excellence.

◆ *My dad showed his support and appreciation for my budding art career when I was nine years old. My mom was a chronic complainer about the mess I would make with my art work and supplies. My dad surprised me one day when he took me out to the garage. He had built me an art studio. He helped me to carry all of my supplies, and together we created a space for me to work. He built me a work table and shelving that held all my odds and ends. When I was working on some new art project, my dad would come into my art studio and watch me work. He was always ready to give me advice and make suggestions. I remember my dad's willingness to enter into my childhood fascinations. I had a great dad. He was my ego booster when I needed someone to help me get energized. Today, I still have an art studio, though it's on the twenty-eighth floor of a Manhattan skyscraper. I've come a long way from that garage. I owe my success to my dad, who championed me along the way.*

Dominant Fathering Qualities

◆ *My dad was known as the best auto mechanic in the city. He could work on any kind of car. He had such a curiosity and ability to explore and research. Any time I had a problem, my dad would work with me just like he would a car. The one thing my dad always did was to keep me on the task at hand. He was there if I needed some reassurance, but he never did the work for me. I could ask any questions or raise any concerns and my dad would patiently explain. There were no stupid questions according to my dad. I never felt ashamed to wonder, question, or doubt.*

◆ *I always wanted to be like my father. I admired him as an honest and just man. He was gifted with gentleness and sensitivity. My father was a dentist. Today I am a dentist also. My dad genuinely cared for people. He would donate one day a week to the inner-city dental clinic. I went with him a few times. I saw people there who really scared me. As a white middle-class boy, I had little experience with the black community. Many of my father's clients in this area lived on the streets. My father always smiled at them, shook their hands, and cared for them with unconditional empathy and genuine concern, even those who were drunk or crazy. My fa-*

ther tried to provide them with the best possible dental care. Even today, I try to share my profession with those who can't afford dental care. I want to become more like my father. I want to become known for my willingness to help others and to share my time and talent with those less fortunate.

The champion father can at times be described by his son as one who is bigger than life. Because of his life's accomplishments, the champion father receives admiration and adulation from his son. He may become an image and an example for his son's hopes for the future. The champion father typically receives affection and respect from others. Because he is a man without shame or guilt, he does not apologize for his success, nor does he withdraw from public exposure. The champion father encourages his own son to enjoy the benefits of success and accomplishment. He teaches his son by using both personal example and words of encouragement and affirmation to build his son's self-esteem and confidence.

This fathering style is one that promotes a son's abilities. The champion father does not hold back from correcting nor from using criticism for the sake of his son's personal growth and development. When it is appropriate, he will admonish his son and correct him, while focusing this parental discipline on improvement, understanding, and insight. The champion father also supports his son during difficult times of trials and tribulations without placating or absorbing his son's pain and suffering. This doesn't mean that the champion father stands idle, watching his son struggle. Rather, he continues to challenge his son, while at the same time he promotes his cause. By sharing in his son's dream, the champion father encourages his son toward accomplishing his goals.

The champion father has a discerning heart. He senses the subtle needs of his son and he can anticipate his son's hopes and desires. He helps his son to articulate and to live out his values, beliefs, hopes, and dreams.

The champion father teaches his son by example. This father is seriously committed to a career, hobby, or vocation. In this commitment, the champion father shows a great deal of stamina, perseverance, and dedication to excellence. He models for his son the attitudes and values that communicate personal belief. This mental stamina serves as a role model for the son to emulate.

- *He taught me how to maintain an attitude of personal success. My dad would become so engrossed in his work and hobbies that I would watch in wonder and awe. His skills as an artist were beyond description. I would come into his studio and be entertained for hours by my dad's enthrallment by a new project. Any time I wanted to join in, he would let me. I could work along with my dad or move off in my own direction. Today I have become a very successful commercial artist. I received the drive to excel, explore, and adventure by watching my dad.*

- *My father was a professional football player. Our entire family would enjoy my dad's career during the good and bad times. We got to travel a lot because of my dad's work. Even though my father's career took a lot of family time and attention, he would always include us in his success. I remember my dad talking to one sports television interviewer. Whenever my dad had a chance, he would talk about how proud he was of us kids and how much he loved his wife. My dad taught me well that a career doesn't have to come at the expense of a family or marriage. Today, I rely on those past moments to reassure me when I try to balance home life with work and marriage.*

The champion father is successful and well respected for his achievements. What is even more admirable is the champion father's ability to balance his private and professional life without sacrificing one for the other. He is capable of encouraging his son to enjoy the success of his own career, yet he doesn't make his son feel obligated to follow in his footsteps. The sons who do share in the champion father's career or who develop a career similar to their father's will continue to develop a unique style of their own. They usually are proud to be known as their father's son.

Chapter 9

THE MYSTIC FATHER

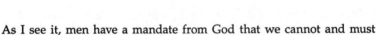

As I see it, men have a mandate from God that we cannot and must not abdicate — to be healers of the world's misery, bearers of His standards, heralds of His word.
> —Leonard E. LeSourd, *Strong Men, Weak Men*

- *My dad was like the absent-minded professor. He was brilliant in math and science, yet dangerous with a hammer or screwdriver. My dad was a great thinker and helped me to see the bigger picture of most of my life events.*

- *I watched him work with the earth. During the planting season, he would become enchanted with the earth, the rain, and the change of seasons. I realized at an early age that my dad walked to the beat of a different drummer.*

- *We raised thoroughbred horses for a living. My dad knew their thoughts. He never beat them or yelled at them. He would talk to the horses, and they seemed to listened. Local horse breeders would come over frequently to ask my dad all kinds of questions. He was almost always right about what a horse needed or wanted or how they were to be treated to get their cooperation.*

- *He never went beyond the eighth grade. Yet my dad had such a wonderful understanding about life, people, and problems. I loved talking with him about my struggles in life. He always had these simple little stories and lessons about life. He talked in parables and would let people come to their own understanding.*

- *My dad was a missionary. He believed in the goodness of humankind. I remember our time in Africa. My dad spent hours listening to the pain and problems of the chief elders as they described how the white man came to take away their forest. Within a few weeks of our stay with this tribe, my dad taught them reforestation and land recovery. Today the tribe calls their baby forest, "Trevor's trees." (My dad's first name is Trevor.) My dad helped this tribe to see beyond their pain and problems. He has a gift for seeing the larger picture and helping others to move toward their dreams and hopes.*

Primary Expressions

The mystic father has faith in his son. He offers his affection through signs and symbols. Some important exchanges between the mystic father and his son are sharing travels, adventures, lessons of life, and responsibility for stewardship of the earth.

The son is willing to journey with his mystic father with a sense of wonder and awe. In the presence of his mystic father a son comes to respect mystery, paradox, and parables as a part of the learning process. The mystic father teaches his son *who* he is in relation to *what* he does. The son learns how this relationship impacts the world about him. When the son shares in his father's dreams and the vision of life, there is a wealth of information and understanding exchanged between father and son. The mystic father is ritualistic with his affections toward his son. He provides his son with unique experiences through sharing of questions, stories, and the communication of family traditions. Passing on to his son the family secrets and stories is an important ingredient of the father-son bonding.

- *My grandfather raised me. My mom and dad died in a car accident when I was two years old. Every day, around 5:30 p.m., my grandpa would go into a small room upstairs on the second floor. No one could accompany him. I was told by grandma that this was grandfather's special place. When I was seven years old, my grandfather invited me to join him in this room. I walked in only to find three things in the room; two chairs and a Bible. I took one chair and grandpa took the other. He told me that this was the time when he would ask the Lord questions and raise concerns about his life. He would study the Bible in order to help himself understand. If the Bible didn't help him find the answer, he would then talk to the empty chair. He would ask God to come and sit with him and help him to find answers to his questions.*

My grandpa wanted me to know that I could come into this room anytime and talk with God about my questions and concerns. If I wanted him to come along for company, that would be okay. For years, grandpa and I would talk with one another about what puzzled us. Sometimes we would find the answer in the Bible, and sometimes we would ask God to talk loud enough for us both to hear and understand. Sometimes God did; and sometimes God left us in our silence. At those times, the answer would well up from within one or both of us. Grandpa taught me about God, prayer, and listening. He was a good man.

♦ *My favorite times were after school when I would find my dad working in the garden. He would share with me what he had learned that day about the earth, plants, gardening, and life in general. We would explore all the new buds and potential fruits and vegetables. For hours we would compare notes on what we had learned from the day — he from the farm and me from my school work. My dad would show me some of his favorite gardening secrets. People from all over the county would come to ask my dad about his gardening techniques. He gave them only enough information for them to want more. My dad was ingenious about making gardens grow to their maximum potential. Even during a dry season, my dad's garden would look the best in the county and grow the most produce. I felt special when my dad shared with me his garden secrets. Even today, I have the best vegetable and flower garden in the city. My dad's secrets are kept alive and well through me. I can't wait to share them with my son.*

Personal Values

The mystic father maintains a cosmic awareness about life, family, and the world community. Through his own lifestyle, he demonstrates a gentle stewardship for the earth and the material goods he collects throughout his lifetime. He appreciates and cares for his possessions. This is why he is able to pass on to his sons and grandsons some of his most prized treasures. He does not hoard his possessions but rather protects what is his with gentle but firm care.

The mystic father has a special intuitive ability. He knows that much of his personal knowledge comes from intuition, and he can access this unconscious part of himself with ease and comfort. The mystic father understands life's mysteries without having formal learning. His understanding of life comes from deep within himself.

- *My younger sister was born with a serious speech impediment. She would mumble with the hope of being understood. If we didn't understand her after the second or third attempt to communicate, she would begin to scream and fly into a temper tantrum. My mother and siblings would be beside themselves when they were trying to figure out what she wanted. The redeeming moment came when my dad would intervene. He would always understand what she wanted. It was truly amazing. My dad said that we should not just listen to her mumbling or try to figure out what her head was trying to say. Instead, we needed to look into her eyes; then we would understand what her heart was saying.*

- *My mystic father was a very successful businessman. He owned warehouses throughout the city. One day he was inspecting an empty building downtown in the inner city. He came upon three homeless adults. They had built little bedrooms out of cardboard boxes to stay warm. My dad was haunted by that scene. He began to offer housing for homeless people throughout the city. A conflict came about one day when a warehouse that was full of homeless people was needed to store items that had just arrived at the dock. My dad decided to keep the homeless people in the warehouse because of an impending winter storm. When the distributors heard of this decision, they became enraged. They claimed that this was bad business management and that such an attitude could jeopardize their inventory and future sales.*

  That same day, my dad came home and shared with me his decision. I was twelve years old at the time. I thought that what he did was heroic; I told him so. He said that because I was willing to help him see his true values he would let the Lord take care of his distributors. That evening, my dad received a phone call from a company that was just opening up three new stores. They needed immediate supplies from the very merchandise my dad had waiting at the docks. Within four hours, the deal was complete. My dad made a small fortune from that company; and the homeless people had a place to stay. That night we got thirty-six inches of snow. My dad saved people's lives because of his kindness toward the homeless.

Primary Virtue

Hospitality is a primary virtue of the mystic father. He has the ability to care for many people. His kindness and sensitivity models for his son that much may be gained in life through respect, gentleness, and an open heart.

- *My dad could never walk by a street beggar and not give him some change and a fine compliment. For years, I watched how unconditional was my father's love for all men and women. Today I am a social worker, and I pray daily that I have the kind of loving heart my dad had for people.*

The mystic father has the ability to welcome new ideas and new adventures with a spirit of wonder. He is not limited by his own sense of history or personal experiences. He encourages his son to be open to the unpredictable forces of life. A welcome attitude toward surprise, the unexpected, risks, and experimentation are all a part of the virtue of the mystic father.

- *My dad would always preface a new experience with, "Well, son, we've never done this before. Let's go for the gusto." He never hesitated to try something different or new. He had an insatiable appetite for exploration. He taught me by his own example that life is an adventure and that we ride with the waves.*

- *I never did know my real father. My adopted father is a Catholic priest. He's white and I'm black. He works in a state prison. I have gone to work with him. I watched him work with the hardest of criminals, always with a firm but kind heart. He would tell me that these murderers and rapists were not really bad men. They just needed a lot of tough love and firmness. My dad never let the racial issues get in the way of his caring for those inmates, most of whom were black. I admire him and grew to love him for his vast abilities to care for anyone who came across his path.*

The mystic father tends to commit himself to a cause or a quest. He values the big picture of life but doesn't forget the smaller pieces to the puzzle. He is at home in the world of spirituality, yet he may not subscribe to any one kind of religion. The mystic father invites his son into mysticism. His mysticism is experienced mostly through a sensitivity to creation and to care for the earth and its environment.

Divine Idea

♦ *My dad almost had a heart attack when he saw me and my friends trying to build a tree fort. He came running outside crying, "Don't hurt that tree anymore." He helped us quickly remove the nails we had pounded into the tree in order to hold up the foundations of our fort. My dad then helped us design a tree fort that didn't use nails. He showed us how to use ropes and stilts to support the tree fort. That way, the tree would not be hurt in any way. I remember the look of relief on my dad's face when we pulled that last nail out. I can still see him talking to that tree. "They didn't really mean to hurt you," he said to the tree. "I'm sorry if they did hurt you. I know that they will learn a great deal from you if they can hang around you and play." My dad taught me how to respect the forest and nature in general. I grew to love him for his kindness toward all of creation.*

The mystic father is illustrated in a wonderful book by Howard Pyle, *The Garden Behind the Moon*. It is an allegory about David, a lonely young boy who is ridiculed as a dumb-witted "mooncalf."

David meets up with Hans Krout, a cobbler and mystic father. People of the village used to say about Hans that he knew less than nothing. "Yet in spite of what folks said, Hans Krout did know something. He knew more about the moon-path, and the Moon-Angel, and the moon, itself, than almost anybody." Hans Krout teaches David about the secret of walking up to the glimmering path across the waves of light on the ocean to discover the beautiful happy garden behind the moon. As David learns to pass behind the Moon-Angel, he also passes into manhood and starts a hero's journey to bring lost treasures back to earth.

Typical of the mystic father, Hans introduces his son and other boys into a world of wonder and awe. He ushers his son into a profound awareness of his own giftedness and of the gifts of the world within him and about him. The mystic father teaches his son a profound respect for the divine, the holy, and the natural.

If the mystic father forgets or neglects his own connection to the earth and to other adult relationships, he can overwhelm his son with too much information and insight. With too much stress on information rather than formation, the son may become stressed and tense. Instead of feeling his father's enthusiasm for the unexplored and unknown, the son may experience rifts of anxiety and fear. If the mystic father does not temper his revelations with sensitivity to what his son can absorb, he may put his son into states of panic, fear, and distress.

♦ *My dad was on the front lines of the black people's movement. He would picket, get arrested, lose his job, stage planning sessions in our home, and talk for hours about his ideas for a new freedom for black people. I would try to get caught up in his stories and try to share his enthusiasm, but most times I would just freeze up inside. Many times I felt like I was in a wind storm. I wanted to be with my dad when he marched or picketed, but I wasn't allowed to go because my mom felt it was dangerous. I would wait up most of the night until I heard of my dad's situation. Were we going to have to go downtown to bail him out, or was he going to bring home more adventure stories that would pump me up with excitement and fear?*

I believed in my dad's work and dreams. I realize now that if I had been involved with my dad's picketing, I couldn't have handled all that excitement. My dad's excitement that he did share with me turned me into a bowl of anxiety. Looking back now, I don't think my dad should have shared as much with me as he did.

The mystic father is one of the faces in *The Chosen.* Reubin's father is a scholar, writer, and teacher who publishes articles and gives talks around the country advocating the new state of Israel. A single parent, he has to balance his time between maintaining a job, advocating the cause for Israel, and being a father to Reubin. Reubin tries to share in his father's work through his involvement with an underground movement that ships guns and ammunition to the war-torn country of the Jews. Reubin's father is so taken up in his work that he doesn't notice his son's desire to share in his efforts. One morning, Reubin comes home after being out all night helping to load weapons on a freighter. His father is very upset with him for being away all night. The two of them have an argument about where Reubin is spending all his time. Reubin confesses his activities and explains how he is trying to help his father fulfill his dream. Reubin and his father discuss their differences over breakfast. The ability of Reubin's father to listen to his son and to talk about their differences is a wonderful example of a healthy mystic father.

In the movie *Indiana Jones and the Last Crusade* we see a model of the mystic father-and-son relationship. Sean Connery epitomizes the image of the mystic father who has lost touch with his son's need for a healthy father-son relationship. The beginning of the movie illustrates the absolute freedom that the son of a mystic father may have if the father is not grounded in his son's day-to-day needs, but this freedom is a mixed blessing indeed. After years of estrangement, Indiana is reunited with his father. As they attempt escape from Nazi Germany in a helium transport, Indiana says to his father, "Do you remember the last time we had a quiet drink? Huh? I had a milk shake?"

His father, deeply engrossed in his diary, which details his lifelong quest for the Holy Grail, replies, "Hum, what are you talking about?"

"We didn't talk," Indiana says. "We never talked."

"Do I detect a rebuke?" asks his father.

Indiana replies, "A regret. It was just the two of us. It was a lonely way to grow up. It must have been lonely for you, too, Dad. Why couldn't you be like the other dads...?"

"Actually," argues Indiana's father, "I was a wonderful father. Did I ever tell you to eat up, go to bed, wash your ears? I respected your privacy. I taught you self-reliance."

"What you taught me," replies Indiana, "was that I was less important to you than people who died five hundred years ago in another country!"

Indiana's father initially defends himself but concludes his explanation with, "But I'm here now, son. What do you want to talk about now?" Indiana's struggle to begin a discussion sputters into speechlessness.

This segment of the movie illustrates very well how the mystic father may become lost in his own dreams and discoveries and thus lose sight of his son's need for his personal attention. The mystic father attempts to provide freedom and space for his son in hopes that the boy will develop a sense of self-reliance. The danger, however, is to be found in the perception that the son of a mystic father may have regarding this freedom and space. He may very well perceive this much freedom as an absence of interest or concern on the part of his father.

Relational Style

The mystic father expresses care for his son by sharing his wisdom and personal understanding of the world about him. He shares with his son the intimate moments he has experienced whenever he is one with the earth. The father's dreams and beliefs are part of his personal relationship with his son. Dreams, life's purpose and meaning, wonder about the world, design about the future, and recollection about the past are all important to this father-son relationship.

There remains a simplicity about how the mystic father cares for his son. The fond affection established between father and son allow them to enjoy simple and obvious life experiences, moments that to some people would appear to be boring and dull. Some typical ways for the mystic father to relate to his son are watching a sunset together, walking quietly side by side, attending church or a retreat together, rocking on the front porch swing, or just spending time reminiscing.

Dominant Fathering Qualities

The mystic father teaches his son gratitude and respect. They enjoy the simple things of life in special and sacred moments. The mystic father opens his son's senses to reasonable, purposeful, and meaningful living.

- *I got caught up in my father's dream. He was an engineer. He would come home at night and we would spend hours building, constructing, and designing the perfect city. We would draw a variety of plans. Then we would share our thoughts and imagine how we could create a city that would not hurt the environment and yet would allow us to enjoy the comforts of the twenty-first century. My dad would share with me his concerns about pollution, recycling, and global warming. We would share our ideas about how to how to solve these problems. One time my dad came up with the idea of working with companies who could benefit from recycling. We began to design recycling plants and products that could come from such efforts. Today, I work for a recycling company. Many of my dad's ideas are the backbone to our company's financial success. My dad continues to enjoy inventing, exploring, and imagining. He is my primary consultant. He has never asked for recognition or acknowledgement for his contributions to recycling or to my company's success. I could never have become this successful without my dad's ideas and imagination.*

The mystic father draws his son into the world of imagination, imagineering, wonder, and awe. He is comfortable working in the world of symbols and the unconscious. He reminds his son how important it is to be a bridge between what was, what is, and what could be. The mystic father is quick to remind his son of the wider implications of his life choices. This fathering style promotes a son's awareness of consequences, possibilities, options, and further quests. Important dynamics to this father-son relationship are reflection, meditation, consideration, and wondering.

Chapter 10

THE MENTOR FATHER

———————— ✎ ————————

A father can aid in this process by helping his son to become independent from him as early as possible, and using himself as a visible role model in explaining how the world works. The father should be supportive and on call for advice when it is requested, providing rescue service for his son only when the situation warrants such action. Through this kind of communication a constructive rather than a destructive relationship can be established between father and son.

—Lewis Yablonsky, *Fathers and Sons*

- *I remember going to work with my dad and watching everything he did. He let me try each of the machines and tools that could be handled by a small kid like myself. My dad let me experiment with different ways to work with the tools of his construction trade. He was always direct, kind, and firm, yet understanding. Today I still like working with my dad. He is still someone I admire. I still perceive him as someone knowing a little bit more than me about the career we have in common.*

- *I could always talk to my dad about life struggles. He would give me options to consider: he never gave me just one answer. He always wanted me to take personal responsibility for my decisions. It was okay to make a mistake. You just had to own it and learn from it.*

- *My father was a hard worker. He grew seed potatoes. I worked by his side and would listen to him talk about what he learned from a magazine he read or from a book that captivated him. My dad*

130

talked to me as though I had a lot of abilities and strengths. Today we both run the farm, and I see my father more than ever as a kind and wise person.

- *I got along well with my pop. He was very much absorbed in his business as a distributor of paper goods. We would drive together and I would help him make his deliveries. Today his business has grown so big that he now works exclusively out of the main office. My pop is always eager to share with me how to develop my own small company. We talk a lot on the phone. My pop is my best consultant.*

- *I have always considered my father as my best and personal confidant. He would give me his undivided attention when I had a question or problem. My best times with my dad were when we both got up early in the morning and made breakfast with each other. I miss my dad. He died a couple of years ago. Now I enjoy making breakfast for my son. This is our special time together.*

Primary Expressions

The mentor father has a great capacity for empathy. He has the ability to hear what is being said and to extract deeper feelings and concerns from his son. Most mentor fathers include their sons in their work experiences. Spending time side by side in the work place is a necessary element of this relationship.

- *My dad taught me how to do it my own way. Not that I wasn't to be open to other people's ideas. It was important to my dad that I took ownership for my work. Being proud of what I do keeps me interested and motivated. I always have felt that I was an apprentice to my dad. Even today I see him as someone always learning, open to new experiences, and wanting to share these experiences with me and our friends.*

The mentor father encourages his son to discover his personal pathway to success. He is concerned that his son develop his own style, expression, and skill.

- *My dad was a surgeon. His dad was a surgeon. My great grandpa was a country doctor. Today, I'm studying to become a surgeon.*

My friends tease me that I am caught in a web of generational du-
plication. I want to be like my father. I call my dad a lot to consult
with him about my course work. He is a great teacher and shows
a lot of interest in what I am doing. I have never felt equal to my
dad nor thought of myself as his peer. I'm not sure if that is bad or
not. I do feel secure in knowing that my dad has more experience
than I do, and I can rely on his wisdom.

The mentor father typically has accomplished most of his life's goals and is now willing to pass on to the next generation what he has learned. He is perceived as more experienced if not more intelligent than his son. He is willing to work with his son as the boy learns how to achieve his life goals. The mentor father provides consultation, advice, and a willingness to correct and admonish if he perceives that his son is not living out his own personal values. The mentor father uses himself as a teaching model for what can be achieved in life. Many times, the son of a mentor father wants to model his life choices after his father's.

Personal Values

Learning from personal experiences is most important to the mentor father. Firsthand experience is the best way to provide a sense of ownership and confidence. The primary concern of the mentor father is to build self-esteem in his son and to help him achieve his dream. The mentor father who has achieved his own goals wants to share the fruit of his work with his son. He wants to pass on his secrets for success, his badge of excellence, and his belief in his son's potential and goodness.

The mentor father maintains an openness to learn and to explore. However, he is selective about how he spends his time. He concentrates enthusiastically on his career, lifestyle, and life expressions. The mentor father remains open to collecting new data and to sharing his new discoveries with others.

This fathering style usually adopts other men outside of the family system. The mentor father will care for and guide other males. Such guidance might include mentoring a younger male in the business world by helping him through school. The mentor father and his apprentice maintain an unequal relationship. The son or other adopted male acknowledges the mentor father as one who is more intelligent, experienced, wise, and secure.

Primary Virtue

The mentor father has personal confidence and stamina. He reflects an air of security and strength. He is usually admired by others for his self-esteem. Yet he is able to acknowledge his own limitations and can defer to others who have greater competency. The mentor father can ask for help without feeling insecure. He teaches his son by example. Therefore the mentor father and son need to spend quality time together working, exploring, discussing, and sharing common experiences. The son will learn from his father's behavior.

+ *I watched my father listen with such intensity when the doctor tried to explain how to feed my mother through the feeding tube. It was at that moment that I realized my father didn't know everything. I always perceived him as all-knowing and brilliant. Now as he watched with fear and concern, I saw another side of my father's wisdom. He could ask for help. He could admit his limitations. He showed no embarrassment with knowing that he didn't know how to work with the feeding tube. When the doctor left, he and I went into the kitchen. My father began to share with me how intimidated and fearful he was about feeding my mother. It was then that I realized that to be wise meant that you could admit that you didn't know everything and you didn't have to feel badly about it either.*

Divine Idea

+ *My father had a special saying that he taught to all six of his kids: "If you don't know how to do a thing, then ask for a little help. It takes more intelligence to admit that you don't know something than to brag about what you do know."*

The mentor father encourages his son to remain open to dialogue with others. He encourages his son to use good sense to learn and to know what works best for him. It is typical for the mentor father's son to ask himself how his father would answer his questions. "What would Dad say about this?" or "What would Dad do in a situation like this?" The mentor father becomes an interior guide for his son. The son becomes stronger and more capable by learning to defer to his father's consultations. The son learns that it is okay to know his limits and to rely on others for what may be lacking in himself. There is no need for apology when it comes to weaknesses or limitations.

Forrest Carter's book *The Education of Little Tree* illustrates the model of the mentor father. From the age of four or five Carter was inseparable from his part-Cherokee grandfather, who owned a farm and ran a country store. Grandpa called him Little Sprout; when he grew taller, he became Little Tree. From Grandpa he absorbed the Cherokee ethic: to give love without expecting gratitude, to take from the land only what you need. Little Tree watches a mountain storm when nature is birthing spring, learns bird signs and wind songs and which crops to plant by the dark of the moon. Little Tree is mentored by his grandpa. He learns with a growing humility about the human condition and the wonders of earth's treasures. Grandpa teaches Little Tree how to receive from the earth and how to work respectfully with both nature and humans. Grandpa also gives Little Tree the space to learn from his experiences. He instructs his grandson that even mistakes are opportunities to grow and learn.

In the movie *The Man Without a Face,* Mel Gibson portrays the mentor fathering style as a teacher. Chuck Norstadt, a young boy trying to live his life with a mother and two half-sisters, is desperate for male companionship. To escape from this home situation, Chuck hopes to pass a placement exam and to enter a military academy. One night Chuck dreams that he is in a military parade. He is held on the shoulders of two men, surrounded by male graduates, and escorted by a beautiful woman. On the sidelines are other beautiful women admiring him and cheering for him. In the crowd is his mother with her fourth or fifth husband and his two half-sisters. The older sister has her mouth taped, and the younger is without the braces she wears in real life. Following behind the parade are all the ex-husbands of his mother, Chuck's former stepfathers. As Chuck enjoys this fantasy, he begins to realize that there is a face he cannot see at the edge of the crowd. The dream begins to fade and the cheering crowd turns silent. Suddenly, everyone begins to stare at Chuck with disapproval. Then Chuck awakes from his dream.

Eventually, Chuck gets acquainted with his new home and neighborhood and meets Justin McCloud. Mr. McCloud is a burn victim, his deformity a result of a car accident. Chuck learns that Mr. McCloud was a teacher for the entrance exams for the military school.

Chuck admits to Mr. McCloud that he is sick and tired of living with three females. So Mr. McCloud cautiously accepts the task of tutoring Chuck for the entrance exams. In his wisdom, Mr. McCloud assigns Chuck the task of digging various holes and then filling them. Mr. McCloud uses his expertise to help Chuck develop a sense of self. In time, the two become intimate friends and Chuck eventually claims Mr. McCloud as his tutor and best friend.

As the plot develops, Chuck discovers that his biological father committed suicide in a psychiatric ward. He runs to Mr. McCloud and seeks comfort. Unfortunately, many innuendoes have been circulating about Mr. McCloud's past. Chuck's mom begins to suggest that Mr. McCloud could be sexually involved with her son. These suggestions lead to a domino effect of gossip and slander, and the tutorial work between Chuck and Mr. McCloud is terminated. Later, an investigation is made by some officials of this little town that insinuate misbehavior on the part of Mr. McCloud. All contact between Mr. McCloud and Chuck is ended, and the personal relationship between them is forbidden.

Although the events of this plot may appear tragic, the ending to the story focuses on the wonderful mentor father Mr. McCloud and his relationship with Chuck. Because of Chuck's tutorial work with Mr. McCloud, he passes his entrance exams for the military academy. The highlight of the movie is Chuck's graduation, which again evokes the dream scenario. This time, however, the face at the edge of the crowd is *not* invisible. It is, in fact, Mr. McCloud, his presence quietly affirming him. Mr. McCloud also reclaims his wonderful gift of teacher and mentor and begins his life in another town. The movie is superb in its illustration of mutual benefits received by both the mentor father and his son. It also confirms that many men have the opportunity to mentor men other than their sons, and together they will reap the fruits of intimacy, trust, and friendship.

Relational Style

The mentor father desires to pass on to his son the success and knowledge of his own lifetime. Sharing learned experiences and stories of success becomes important to the mentor father-son relationship. The son's admiration dominates the relationship because the relationship is perceived as unequal in knowledge and life experiences. The mentor father can be blunt, probing, and objective about his opinions. He adopts his son's causes and explores with him possibilities and options. The mentor father does not participate equally with his son in the accomplishments of work. He stands back and allows his son to engage fully in his tasks. He waits to reflect with his son on the wisdom gleaned from these experiences.

The mentor father reflects in retrospect about his son's educational experiences. He helps to evaluate, review, and critique. Making corrections and pointing out both the strengths and the weaknesses of various events occur in intense and intimate encounters in the father-son relationship. The mentor father teaches his son how to be independent without isolating himself from those who nurture and care for him. He also shows his son how to enjoy autonomy without becoming arrogant or competitive. The mentor father keeps a certain amount of emotional distance from his son. This is done not to withdraw himself, but to teach his son how to maintain and contain himself. When the mentor father reveals his personal side, there is a generous amount of emotion and affection. The mentor father maintains a certain formality with his son in the public forum. He wants his son to enjoy the benefits of personal success, responsibility, and self-management.

Dominant Fathering Qualities

The mentor father proclaims his belief in his son's abilities. He comes to recognize his son's gifts and can personally reflect upon them with him. The mentor father encourages his son to borrow from his father's experiences. Teaching by example, the mentor father invites his son to wonder, critique, and ponder what he sees and understands. Critical reflection and review are an important part of this father-son relationship. The mentor father has enough ego strength to let his son practice his skills on him. He becomes a sounding board for many of his son's life events. The mentor father acts as a clean mirror reflecting back the unknown or unloved content of his son's experiences.

- *I went through a terrible time during the 1960s. I was into just about anything that was bad or unhealthy. My dad stood by, watching and waiting for me to come around. In retrospect, nothing that my dad could have said or done would have entered my frame of reference. My dad's willingness to wait for me to begin to change makes him a hero in my life. When I was ready to talk, he was ready to listen. He never held back his opinion and didn't ignore mine. We had some really heavy conversations that sometimes ended in silence because we had reached an impasse. My dad never walked away. I walked a lot.*

- *I can remember my dad watching me struggle with putting my car together. I had to replace the head on the engine. He offered to help, but I wanted to do it myself. He sat on the porch as though he knew I would dig a hole for myself that I couldn't get out of. He was so sensitive to my moodiness and offered assistance only when I asked for it. I could sense that he wanted me to succeed with this task and come out the other side as more confident. He sat there all day. When I asked for help he gave it to me. Then he left me alone until I needed more information or assistance. My dad, by the way, is an expert mechanic. I'm glad he let me learn from my struggles and helped me only when it seemed impossible for me.*

* *My father was an upright and good man. He lived his life according to his values. I was hanging out with a bunch of guys and we got arrested for breaking into our high school and messing things up. My dad came to the jail. He asked for a private room so he could talk with me. He listened to my story and then reviewed with me what I did right and wrong. He would not let me off the hook for what I did. He reassured me that he was with me and would never leave my side, but I had to pay for the wrong that I did. I can still remember the other fathers. One of them was complaining about the legal system to his son and their lawyer. One father did nothing but yell and scream at his son. He did a thorough job of shaming him in front of all of us. Another father sat there and cried. I could see the pain and embarrassment on my friend's face. My dad was tough on me. He was honest. Yet I knew he would walk with me through this painful mistake of my life.*

The mentor father has an inner wisdom that guides him in his parenting style. He accommodates the needs of his son with sensitivity and firmness. He does not do the work for his son, but guides him and directs him toward his goals. The mentor father has a way of making his son feel smarter than he perceives himself to be. He adopts his son's causes and shares unlimited time, attention, and interest with him. He does not, however, assume his son's responsibilities.

Part Three

WHERE DO I BEGIN?

Chapter 11

Inner Work

——————— ୡ ———————

In their book *King, Warrior, Magician, Lover,* Moore and Gillette remind men:

> We need to learn to love and be loved by the mature masculine. We need to learn to celebrate authentic masculine power and potency, not only for the sake of our personal well-being as men and for our relationships with others, but also because the crisis in mature masculinity feeds into the global crisis of survival we face as a species. Our dangerous and unstable world urgently needs mature men and mature women if our race is going to go on at all into the future.
>
> Because there is little or no ritual process in our society capable of boosting us from Boy psychology into Man psychology, we each must go on our own (with each other's help and support) to the deep sources of masculine energy potentials that lie within us all. We must find a way of connecting with these sources of empowerment.[1]

Grief

The challenge for men today is to explore ways to access their inner potential and to discover avenues of personal empowerment. One of the most important ways for a man to begin to meet his own fathering needs is to grieve for and reconcile personal losses between his father and himself. The psychological damage that unresolved grief can create is awesome and frightening. A man's well-being can be stifled and seriously damaged by the power of unresolved grief.

Grief is a powerful emotion that infiltrates our biological, psychological, spiritual, and social interactions. Unresolved grief hinders a man from living life to the fullest. His body may grieve and cry for him if he does not do his grief work consciously. The body is designed in such a way that emotions, feelings, and attitudes need to be released through external expressions. If the power and energy of these inner workings are not released, the body can maintain its "holding" pattern only so long. Eventually, the body breaks down or this pent-up energy begins to "poison" the body. A simple lesson for men to keep in mind is this: "Either you spend the energy (grief, anger, fear, anxiety) or the energy will spend you (nightmares, panic attacks, lower back pain, migraine headaches, gastrointestinal disorders)."

It takes greater time, energy, and resources to manage and to contain prolonged grief than does it does to resolve grief in its early stages. Men who prolong their unresolved grief sooner or later resort to fatal tactics. They abuse alcohol and drugs; they indulge in too much or too little food; they suffer from work addiction and various sexual disorders. Often they rage and act out against authority and loved ones. Dependent on outside approval and encouragement, they take life-threatening risks through obsession with exercise and food intake or self-defeating thoughts, feelings, behaviors, and isolation.

These men lack the ability to express their own feelings and their own ideas. They live only in the here-and-now. Although they savor their successes or accomplishments, they are constantly driven to do more, to work harder, and to perform faster. Lacking a sense of humor, they become intolerant of mistakes, others' as well as their own. They are restless, angry, fearful, anxious, unapproachable, with little or no affective expressions. Their mournful attitudes and lethargic and chronic depression often lead to feelings of despair and suicide.

It is my belief that when we encounter a loss and begin the grieving process, this process will continue until one of the three following options is completed: (1) we retrieve the loss; (2) we replace the loss; (3) we surrender the loss.

For some men, the inner work they need to accomplish is to claim a new relationship with their fathers. If their father is still alive, they are able to redesign their attitudes, perceptions, and expectations of their father. Such an attitude adjustment may improve the possibility of a more personal relationship with their father. Some attitudes that men have held toward their fathers hinder the possibility of love and respect for their dads. New father-son interactions may be enabled if men take the responsibility to find healthy expressions and exchanges between themselves and their fathers. Men need to let go of unfair and unrealistic expectations of their fathers. "Many of us seek the generative, affirming, and empowering father (though most of us don't know it), the father who, for most of us, never existed in our actual lives and won't appear, no matter how hard we try to make him appear."[2]

Sam, a participant in a men's group, shared how he came to realize that his father's way of showing him support throughout his life was not the problem. The problem, as Sam now perceives it, was his expectations and the way *he* wanted his father to give him support.

Sam's mom and dad divorced when he was two years old. His mother had been very soft-spoken and had taught Sam social graces that were not part of his father's parenting style. Because his father's behavior appeared to Sam as blunt, crude, and boisterous, Sam failed to notice the subtle underlying encouragement that his dad was really trying to offer him. Once Sam came to realize that he needed to adjust his own perceptions of his father, he began to see beneath his father's so-called crude behaviors. Sam could eventually acknowledge that his father was actually complimenting, encouraging, and affirming him.

In telling his story, Sam said that exchanging affections between people is similar to the way a radio station sends and receives sound waves. Each of us has our particular station through which we receive affection. Sam realized that most of his life he was trying to receive his father's affection on channel two, which is the channel his mother used. His dad, however, was sending affection out on a different channel. Sam accepted the challenge that he could change channels and tune into his father's "sound wave." Now that Sam has been learning to live in his father's world, there is a lot of healing and satisfaction between him and his dad. Sam admits that he would like his father to be more in sync with Sam's sensitivities. However, he realizes that his dad, like all of us, is a limited human being.

His dad probably won't, or can't, change his ways of giving and receiving. But Sam himself has had many opportunities for receiving help, healing, and recovery that his father had not experienced. Sam is at peace with his new attitude of accepting his father and his father's ways of giving attention and affection.

Another option of grief work is to accept that healthy fathering is gone forever and to realize that it cannot be replaced. The inner hunger and yearning for past nurturing can be resolved only by letting go and surrendering the desire for your father's presence. This act of surrender can be achieved through a full and conscious acceptance of the loss.

This means that the loss has been named. It is imperative that you share the loss and its personal meaning with someone you trust. Feeling the emotions that are attached to each loss and letting your body embrace the honest impact of these emotions takes some practice. It is especially difficult if you come from a family system that discourages emotional expressions. This stage of grief work takes time, practice, and energy. You may have to spend some quality time with a particular feeling to grasp its intensity and depth.

You will know that you have let go of the desired loss when you can remember the lost moment and not feel burdened or oppressed by the feelings once attached to it. Then you must decide to hand over any further expectations for having this loss replaced by your father. When a man honestly grieves his losses he will enter into a profound degree of serenity.

Serenity allows a man to move on and not to be controlled by resentment or bitterness because of the past. Serenity frees a man to live in the here-and-now and not to be ruled by memories. This newfound freedom empowers him to seek out new relationships and to deepen those relationships already existing. Freed from his debilitating grief, he can begin to experience joy and a whole wide array of healthy feelings and emotions.

Serenity also opens a man to *simplicity*. He begins to receive satisfaction from those little things that usually get overlooked. A man with simplicity becomes more playful and lighthearted. His desire to reach out and make contact with others to exchange affection and support becomes more pronounced. He can now receive from others and can maintain an attitude of hospitality toward others. He becomes more attuned to nature and the environment around him. Appreciation and gratitude for what he has and is able to share become hallmarks of his newfound freedom.

Solitude

A man is born three times in his life. He is born of his mother, he is born of his father, and finally he is born of his own deepself. The last is the birth of his individuality.[3]

The birthing process for each man can take place only in the depths of solitude and introspection. Moments of time alone provide a man with the space he needs to discover his inner resources. The ability to introspect, which means to look within oneself, provides a man with the opportunity to host memories, stories, and experiences that need to be revisited. This is done so that any unfelt honesty or truth within himself can be touched, embraced, and then integrated.

During these periods of solitude, a man may awaken to those memories that ache for the father's presence. With further exploration of his interior condition, he may discover a large empty space within himself. This space was meant to be filled with father-son memories and moments of the past. Nothing else is permitted to enter into this sacred space.

Daniel, a member of a men's support group, talked about this large black hole he imagined he had in the middle of his chest:

- *When I try to imagine my dad, I feel consumed and swallowed up by this black hole in my chest. Nothing I have tried to do has been comforting. I have tried to fill this space with work, sex, money, accomplishments, even hatred and rage. Nothing seems to fill this hole. Then I heard about a man's need for fathering and that only another man can help to heal this gaping wound in my chest. I need someone strong enough to crawl into this black hole with me and begin to repair it and heal it.*

Daniel was assured that half of what he needed could be provided by the men's group he attended. The other half — how to become the father he needed — he would have to learn for himself.

> Adult sons must be able to mourn their ideal fathers. The mourning process will teach them how to father themselves, how to fill their inner emptiness through creativity. The transition from being a son to being a man involves giving up the ideal father and giving into the ideal itself. The challenge for men with missing fathers is to themselves become the fathers they lacked.[4]

Daniel was given the opportunity to learn from his dreams, archetypes about men and fathering, journaling, imagery, body work, grief and anger work, prayer and meditation, how he could develop fathering skills and begin to creatively nurture himself. It is imperative that men be taught how to listen to their interior world and how to entertain their feelings and emotions, night dreams and nightmares, and their prayer images and imagination. Men must learn how to understand their interior potential and to build a bridge from that interior life to their outer world.

Dreams

Nighttime dreams are echoes of inner truth wrapped up in a package. Each package (that is, symbol) in a dream needs to be unwrapped and displayed. Dreams are a second chance to capture what we overlooked the first time around. The more important, valuable, and life-giving the truth overlooked during daytime living, the greater the emotional impact of the nighttime dream or nightmare.

There are excellent books that can help you to understand dream symbols and to begin dream work. When you begin dream work, you begin a lifetime adventure. You will discover a world of infinite inner truth that lies within each one of us. (See the bibliography for book listing on dreams and dream work, p. 190.)

Temperaments

As you begin to relate to the different fathering styles addressed in this book, it will become essential to your healing process that you understand the variety of temperaments that influence a fathering style. Temperaments are the subtle personality differences that affect how we display ourselves to the outer world. Temperament also includes our consistent actions, likes and dislikes, patterns of behavior, and values. Ways of perceiving, thinking, using feelings, and producing and collecting information are expressions of temperament.

The ten fathering styles offered in this book may be easily extended to include many subtle and various expressions of each temperament type.[5] Understanding how temperament influences and limits our ability to father helps us to gain a greater appreciation of our own fathering style or our father's style of fathering.

Learning about your individual temperament type helps you to grow in tolerance and respect for others. People are different from one another, and these differences will color how a man fathers. The Myers-Briggs Type Indicator (MBTI) is a tool for helping people to identify which temperament type fits their innate personality and directs how they communicate to the outer world who they are and how they act. Life is experienced and processed in many different ways; Myers-Briggs measures contrasting styles in four areas: introvert vs. extravert; sensation vs. intuition; feeling vs. thinking; and judging vs. perceiving.

Certain people choose other people as a source for reviving their personal energy. Those who revive themselves this way we call the "extravert" type. Others have an opposite temperament. People with a temperament type opposite of extravert desire solitude and time alone in order to recover their energy. We call this the "introvert" type. You may be one type and your father the other.

Seventy-five percent of the general population report a preference for a temperament category termed "sensation." Sensation in the MBTI means that people of this temperament prefer to collect their information through and with the senses. They value experiences and the wisdom of the past. Twenty-five percent of the population indicate a preference for "intuition." This means that these people rely on metaphor and imagery as communication tools. People with this characteristic are futuristic in their thinking.

A father who parents using his sensate preference will not connect well with a son who is strong in the intuitive preference. Likewise, the expectations of a son who operates from an intuitive perspective create many challenges for a sensate father.

Men who choose impersonal, analytical, and factual information to make decisions are "thinkers," while the "feelers" use personal, sentimental, and emotional processes for their decision-making. Tension, conflict, and misunderstanding can occur between father and son if they operate from the opposite temperaments. Fathers and sons who learn how each comes to make decisions and to draw conclusions can become empathic, sensitive, and respectful of one another.

There are two other temperament preferences that involve conflicting choices. The preference for closure, product orientation, punctuality, and the settling of things is called "judging." If, on the other hand, you like to keep things open-ended, fluid, spontaneous, and open to new possibilities, you have a temperament called "perceiving." The following example illustrates the differences between "judging" and "perceiving":

- *My dad was always late. He would say that he would pick me up at 4:00 p.m., and I would be there waiting already at 3:45 p.m. He would arrive any time after 4:00 p.m., and I'd get so mad at him. When I was a teenager, I took his behavior as a gesture of disregard for my time and that I was not valuable. Now, since I have studied my dad's temperament profile, I see how different his temperament is from mine. I go back over many of my memories and I rewrite my conclusions. I now understand that I wanted my dad to live life the way I did. I have come to appreciate that my dad's style of doing things is different, not wrong. I have also learned to lighten up a bit and try to take on some of my father's perceiving function.*

Learning about temperament types enhances your ability to understand some of the differences between you and your father, between you and your son. By understanding these differences you can become more effective and sensitive to the needs of others — especially when those needs seem foreign to you, perhaps even hostile to you, and so unlike your own.

Compulsions

Each of the healthy and unhealthy fathering styles involves some level of compulsive behavior. A compulsive behavior is experienced as a basic driving force. This compulsion can be a kind of "hidden sin," where sin is understood as a kind of paralysis or hindrance in becoming one's authentic self.[6]

Those men who identified their father's fathering style as good and helpful still acknowledged that their dad had limitations and weaknesses. Those men who are trying to become better fathers and to develop a fathering style that provides the best care and nurturing for their children need to explore, understand, and discipline their own personal compulsions.

Compulsions may be helpfully understood through the Enneagram, which provides a system of nine types of human personality. Each personality has both a particular gift and a negative compulsion that are ingrained within a person's self-concept and have great influence over a person's behavior. Use of the Enneagram may help us to discover our compulsions, understand their causes, and move in a direction that will help us to overcome these drives. *The Enneagram: A Journey of Self Discovery* is described by its authors in this way:

> [It] is intended to help persons see themselves in the mirror of their minds, especially to see the images of personality distorted by basic attitudes about self. To identify and admit these prevailing "compulsions" is to be open to see life more fully, provided that one is willing to address this "hidden sin" in one's behavior and to look directly to God for healing. Though the Enneagram is not meant to be a panacea for becoming holy, its careful study, preferably connected with making some Enneagram workshops, results in a new self-understanding and practical guidelines for achieving healing. This leads one to a greater personal freedom under the lead of the Spirit.[7]

•

Men who want to begin their inner work and to become better fathers for their sons and for their own self-esteem must set aside quality time to explore their personal potential. I was once asked by a group of men why it takes so long to unlearn and then to relearn new ways of being a father and parent. I asked in return, "How long did it take you to become who you are today? Well, then take the total amount of that time and divide it in half. If it takes you only half the amount of time to unlearn and to learn a new fathering style, then you can take the other half of the unused time and go fishing."

The good news is that it takes far less time to learn a new fathering style and to become a good father than it took to survive the trauma and damage left by unhealthy fathering. I have met men in their late sixties and seventies who just recently began their inner work. They are benefiting from renewed relationships with their sons and grandsons. They can testify to the power of personal healing and recovery.

Chapter 12

Second-Chance Fathers

I have worked with many men who have done exceptional inner work and have been able to reconcile many of their personal needs as male, son, and father. Those who have had a second-chance father have been blessed and empowered. They have plumbed the depths and yet soared into heights of health and well-being.

A second-chance father is a significant male who provides emotional nurturing for a man who isn't his biological son. I learned that such persons exist by listening to a variety of men who spoke about their second chance to receive healthy fathering from a male who had befriended them. Here is one man's story regarding his second-chance father.

Doug had just started a new job at a small business that distributed office furniture. He was on his first delivery to a large firm. Doug was very happy to have landed this job. He had lost many jobs prior to this one because of his drinking and drugging. Mr. Thomas, the building manager, met Doug at the loading ramp. It was at their first meeting that Doug became aware of a powerful feeling between him and Mr. Thomas.

During the unloading of his first shipment of inventory, Doug and Mr. Thomas began to talk about Doug's new job. Doug remembers how happy he was and how proud he was of himself. He wanted very much to share his success with someone. Mr. Thomas, in his wisdom, seemed to have sensed how hard Doug had worked to arrive at this point in his career, so he listened to Doug's story. After Doug had completed his delivery, Mr. Thomas said to him, "Doug, I'm proud of you for your new career accomplishment. Come by tomorrow and we'll have lunch together to celebrate your second day on the job."

Doug has known Mr. Thomas now for six years. He still refers to him as Mr. Thomas because of the respect he has for this man. Since that time, Doug has visited with Mr. Thomas often. He defers to this older man in many of his career decisions, life choices, personal relationships, and financial matters. Doug shared with us that Mr. Thomas gave him a feeling of worth and importance. Mr. Thomas has brought Doug into his family to the point that Doug often refers to the Thomas children as his foster brothers and sisters.

In her book *Fathers and Mothers,* Patricia Berry suggests that sons who have not received adequate fathering and nurturing from a significant male will have what she calls "father-hunger." "Hunger" is a very apt term. A healthy body needs salt, water, and protein just as a starving person's digestive tract needs these elements. If it finds none, the stomach will eventually eat up the muscles themselves. Poorly fathered men hang around older men much as the homeless hang around a soup kitchen. Like the homeless, they feel shame over their condition, a nameless, bitter, unexpungeable shame. Women — no matter how much they sympathize with their starving sons — cannot replace that missing substance. Many contemporary sons recognize their father-hunger that no one knows how to satisfy.[1] Guy Corneau agrees:

The patriarchal social system that allowed previous generations of men to stand tall and proud has been widely discredited. Initiation rites no longer exist. The hunger for a father's presence still remains in us though. We realize we have unresolved problems of identity, but the only solution we ever get from our elders is "Grit your teeth and bear it; it won't last forever." They don't even know what we're talking about. To compensate for our inner emptiness, some of us choose a career our father would approve of; others are lucky enough to find substitute fathers. However we compensate, the fact remains that a deep desire for a father's recognition stays with us for a very long time.[2]

In *The Grown-up Man*, John Friel reassures us,

Please don't trap yourself into a life of misery by saying that you didn't get what you needed from your father when you were little so you are doomed forever. Remember, you can get the fathering you need from any healthy man who is able and willing to give it. In some cases, you can even get it from someone who is younger than you.[3]

I have heard numerous men say that they have discovered their second-chance fathers in their siblings, grandfathers, uncles, teachers, coaches, next-door neighbors, male friends, co-workers, therapists, spiritual directors, and peers in men's support groups. The opportunity for a second-chance father may come from a unique situation or by the choice of the son who is looking to satisfy his father-hunger.

♦ *I had just begun my recovery process and soon discovered that my drinking not only affected my thinking, feeling, and relating to others; it also affected my way of doing business and relating to the business world. I was out to begin a new private practice. I quickly found out, though, that I kept slipping into my old alcoholic ways. I realized that I needed someone to help keep me straight and, more so, someone whom I could ask for advice. Asking for help would be a new adventure for me. I came from a family that taught me, "If you don't know how to do it, don't ask for help. Just fake it." Well, my faking days had caught up to me and now I was sinking fast.*

I attended an AA meeting and had been listening to someone give their recovery story. This man spoke about his stinking thinking and how he needed help with keeping himself straight. He had a difficult time asking for help and had to work hard at opening himself to another. He talked about a man he met who became his second-chance father. This guy was hard and tough on him. But this man's love and concern kept him clean and honest. He also had just begun a private practice and needed a lot of advice about the business world and how to be an honest businessman.

As this man spoke about his experiences, I could imagine myself standing up there repeating every word he said. His story was about me. After this guy finished his talk, I felt myself rise from my chair and walk straight to him. It was as if my feet were in charge of my body. My mind struggled about whether I should ask him to be my mentor. Before I could stop myself, I was asking this man to be my second-chance father. I talked quickly and filled him in on the details of my life. I emphasized how much of my life experiences paralleled his. When I was finished talking, he smiled at me with tears running down his cheeks. I felt really embarrassed.

This man went on to tell me that his second-chance father had just died about a week ago. He was at his deathbed. His second-chance father told him that it was time for him to give someone else all that he had received through their relationship. His second-chance father told him to wait until someone came and asked him to be a second-chance father. That request would be his cue that it was time to begin a new phase in his life.

He and I have been friends now for twelve years. My second-chance father has been tough, yet caring, firm, but loving with me. Through his guidance he has helped me to create a vibrant business. I don't give him all the credit for my success, though. I work hard. When I made a mistake, I ran to my second-chance dad and admitted it. I know the day will come when my second-chance father will no longer be there. Then it will be my turn to pass on to another guy, like myself, what I have received from my second-chance father.

Listed below are some characteristics of a good relationship between a son and a second-chance father. You may find this information helpful in establishing fair expectations between you and a second-chance father, and the day may come when you will be able to share the fruits of your work and recovery. You may become a second-chance father.

Based on the research of Nick Stinnett on what keeps a family together, the list delineates how second-chance fathers and sons can maintain cohesion and emotional bonding. Typically, the second-chance father is more the provider; only later does the son learn how to emulate him.

1. They learn to communicate appreciation for one another. They build one another up psychologically.

2. They arrange their personal schedules so that they can do things together or simply be together.

3. They develop positive communication patterns: they learn to listen and attend to one another, to empathize with each other, to show respect and admiration for one another. They allow conflict and anger to happen but resolve it within an appropriate time. Each learns how to show the other emotion and intimate gestures of affection. They also learn to touch one another with warmth and affection.

4. They develop a high degree of commitment to promoting one another's happiness and welfare. They invest time, money, energy, activities, and interest. They are committed to making memories.

5. They share a spiritual orientation. They share their mutual awareness about their God and their purpose in life. They also share how they are called to care for others and include others in their friendship.

6. They learn to deal positively with crises. They take a proactive stance toward one another. They learn to share resources and trust one another and are committed to maintaining the relationship.[4]

Chapter 13

Men Fathering Men

———————— ॐ ————————

Storytelling

The most common, most helpful, and most pleasurable element of growth and recovery that men have shared in our group is storytelling. With a little help and encouragement from others, all men can share their stories, their lived experiences. Storytelling has been used throughout time. Before the written word, family, community, and world experiences of wisdom and grace were remembered through stories. These were passed on to the next generation by the storytellers.

Stories allow a man to share his collected wisdom. Stories empower and enhance a man's personal knowledge. Both the teller and hearer of stories can touch and can be touched by the truth of a story's message that leaves traces of divine insight and human awe. When a man shares his story, a window is opened to his heart. Storytelling not only passes on a lesson of wonder and wisdom; it also allows something of the teller to be revealed and transposed.

Storytelling heals. By its very nature, storytelling confronts dysfunctional family and societal rules that violate healthy human relationships in our homes, work places, and the world community. Storytelling breaks these vicious and crippling cycles for keeping "secrets" and lying and confronts the three laws of an addictive system: don't talk; don't feel; don't trust.

By revisiting experiences of the past, we begin the process of reconciliation that allows us to embrace grief at its most intimate moments. By remembering our stories, we relive blessed experiences, or, for the first time, feel the pain of wounded memories that previously were too difficult to deal with. When we remember, we relive the past and we embrace the fruit of the past. Doing so helps us to enhance the present. Storytelling allows us to savor and to reminisce about our life experiences.

An old Jewish proverb says, "To remember is to become divine." When we allow ourselves to remember and to revisit our past, we capture those blessings again through storytelling. It can take years of remembering and reminiscing to allow the full effect of some graced moments to come to fruition. Instead of looking to the future for the grace desired, the fulfillment of your desire could be standing before you in an unspoken memory and story.

When we share our stories, we share the wisdom of memories with others. It is not enough that God graces you with insight and wisdom as you learn from your past experiences. The fruit of your knowledge needs to be passed on to the next generation. The wisdom of your personal story should be enjoyed and celebrated for generations to come. How many people have passed through this world and not shared the fruit of their life experiences? Imagine how much of our collected wisdom has been lost because of untold stories.

So what do we men need to talk about? With whom do men need to talk? Men's storytelling might begin with stories about their fathers. Guy Corneau in his book *Absent Fathers, Lost Sons* encourages men to break their fathers' silence:

> Our fathers' silence has become our own. Although we have been inducted into the mafia of hereditary silence, our awareness of the suffering this silence has caused us (and our fathers) should discourage us from passing it on to our own sons. The challenge facing men today is to break this long tradition of male silence. It is perhaps the most truly revolutionary act we can ever accomplish.

Those of us who can should start dialogues with our real fathers, despite the fear, frustration, disappointment, or rejection this may lead to. We must fight against falling into the same silence our fathers did; we must try to bridge the gap; we can begin to heal the terrible division between the abstract, disincarnated minds of men and an increasingly cruel world. The time has come to talk of our vulnerability, our deep needs, our internal violence. The time has come for us to proclaim our visions. The time has come for us to share and show ourselves as we actually are, to open ourselves up and become real in the eyes of the people around us. The time has finally come for us to speak.[1]

Some men may have the chance to share with their fathers and through an exchange of stories may create a new era in their relationship. Some men will discover that their fathers are not able or willing to listen to their stories. It may be that the most these men can receive from their dads are moments of *his* recollections. The need for personal self-disclosure may direct a man into other relationships where he can freely share his thoughts and feelings.

The need for personal self-disclosure may lead a man into a support group or into a men's therapy group. It has been my experience that the level of intensity and personal sharing desired by most men calls for a sacred space and a ritual elder. Mircea Eliade describes this sacred space as an essential element for the rites of initiation to be completed. It is a place where the outside world is sealed off and the exchange of wisdom is made so that a process of transformation can be achieved.

The ritual elder is a man who knows the secret wisdom and is able to lead the process of initiation and guide men through the rites of transformation. The ritual elder is a wise old man who lives out a vision of mature masculinity.[2]

Where do men go to find this sacred space and these ritual elders? Men have the opportunity to create sacred space when they gather together for storytelling. Men who have done their inner work and have been healed by the process will become the ritual elders. When men gather together, they provide the very stuff needed to create a sacred space. Their shared masculinity is the element required. When men can consciously gather together with openness and embrace their masculinity, explore their inner wisdom, and exchange this wisdom with one another, we will witness a new age of healthy, masculine men who are balanced, mature, empowered, and generative fathers.

Louis W. McLeod and Bruce K. Pemberton discovered in their men's group that men confronted various issues such as following as well as leading, being receptive as well as active, letting go as well as being in control, facing homophobia as well as attraction to other men, and acknowledging competitiveness as well as cooperative efforts. In their work they came to see that men were yearning for a qualitatively different relationship with other men.[3]

In their later work with men's groups, McLeod and Pemberton arrived at some important guidelines and implications for men-only therapy groups. First, when women are present in a group, men automatically "play" to the women. In the men-only therapy group, the men first explore their intrapersonal dynamics and later their interpersonal relationships. Without women present, competitiveness is diminished. Second, in a coed group, males tend to turn to females for nourishment. In the men-only therapy group, men model nourishment and intimacy between themselves and begin to see each other as sources of support and nourishment. As men begin to identify and express feelings at their own pace, a camaraderie and excitement grows into a self-perpetuating process. Third, men come to appreciate a nonsexualized intimate relationship with other males. This provides the experience that intimacy can be separated from sexuality with women. Fourth, men can explore their anger and rage with reassurance that they cannot overpower the group. In the men-only group it is easy to provide limit-setting structures in which men can fully experience their rage in a safe setting. It is a unique experience for men to receive support and acceptance of their sadness from other men. Fifth, a men-only therapy group has a uniqueness and power. It is invigorating to be with men as they grow and relate intimately to each other.[4]

The Need to Share Secrets

Many of the men who have come to share their personal stories have sooner or later revealed secrets that have previously hindered them from moving into health and well-being. Harboring their secrets has drained them of energetic lives. These men have longed to put into words the dreaded images that have lingered in their minds and hearts. For some men to let go of the unhealthy fathering they have received or have given, they need a safe place in which to reveal their secrets, sins, and sadness.

Physical or sexual abuse is the secret that has created the most damage. This personal abuse may have taken the forms of ridicule, verbal accusations, physical beatings, taunting, sexual abuse, incest, inappropriate touching, exposure to pornography, rape, or dominance by an older person outside of the family unit.[5] Many men have shared that unresolved sexual traumas of the past inhibit them from becoming healthy in their perceptions of manhood and fatherhood.

Frequently a male survivor feels he must conceal the fact that he was abused for fear that he will be rejected, disdained, or exposed to ridicule. Having internalized the view of victims as being less than human, he is certain that others will view him in the same way. The lack of available information about sexual abuse of male children leads him to imagine that he must face his difficulties alone and that few if any other men share his situation. (Some men who have attempted to receive help have in fact had their problems discounted, ignored, or treated insensitively. This treatment serves as confirmation to them that they are not worthy of respect as men.) Seeing himself as less than a man, the incest survivor may view such "male" attributes and accomplishments as strength, power, and success as beyond his reach.[6]

Many men admit that the original abuse may have ended, but the trauma and paralysis continue in various forms. Men who carry their secret of sexual, physical, or verbal abuse keep their story hidden because they believe that no one will understand. Perhaps in their confused thinking it wasn't really that bad. Perhaps it didn't really happen at all. The fear of retribution if they reveal the abuse, the confusion about what they did to deserve this abuse, and the numbness that serves to hide the depth of the pain carried deep within themselves all prevent the survivors from speaking about their trauma.

One man told this story about his struggle with his newly recalled memories of being sodomized by his father while his two older brothers were forced to watch. His father took all three boys into the basement and demanded their attention. After showing them how to masturbate and to perform oral sex on him and on one another, he then taught them how to be "real men." Anal sex was explained as "the best way to get what you want." Brad explained that for years he could not walk into someone's basement without ending up in a full-blown panic attack.

After he got married, he was unable even to change his son's diaper. As his child moved toward potty training, Brad's fears and anxieties increased to the point where he required treatment and medication. The medicines, however, did not work. Brad heard about a men's group, and out of desperation he decided to join. As Brad began to get deeper into his story about the sexual abuse committed by his father and his brothers, he began to make a connection between his fears and his son. Slowly, as Brad disclosed some of the terrible secrets he had kept within himself, he began to experience some relief from his fears. The more Brad told his story, the less panic and fear he had when caring for his son. With the support of the group, Brad came to realize that he did not have to fear his natural abilities to touch and to be tender with his son. He no longer confused these signs of nurturing with the distortions his father and brothers had passed on to him.

A primary lesson we learn from revealing our secrets is to free ourselves from the misinformation we received in past

MEN FATHERING MEN / 163

abusive experiences. If the secret is kept hidden, then false information is left in control of our distorted values, beliefs, and dreams. With the support of the men's group, Brad was learning how to take charge of his own life and to move in a new direction as father to his son.

Mike Lew encourages men to break their secrecy by talking to somebody: "What is most important in breaking the secrecy is not who is the first one to be told, but that you tell someone. The log jam of silence, fear, and intimidation must be broken. Where you start is less important than that you start." He goes on to say,

> Get into the habit of disclosure. If the actual sexual abuse has ended, the effects remain. Talk about them. You will find someone who can listen. You'll probably be surprised at how much support there really is in the world. Don't worry about getting the story right. All the details aren't necessary. You may not even know them yourself. What is important is starting the process, reaching out to someone. It is good enough to tell someone, "Something happened to me." If that is all you know for certain — or if that is all you're able to say — then it's enough for now. If you don't know that much, it is enough for now. If you don't know that much, it is enough to say, "It feels like something could have happened to me." Just once. Once the first log or two starts to move, it is amazing how quickly the others follow until finally the jam has broken up completely and the logs flow easily.
>
> Once the silence is broken — and you see that the world has not ended — it is important to maintain the momentum. Tell your story again and again. Repeating your story:
>
> 1. Makes it more real to you.
>
> 2. Underscores the fact that it is important.
>
> 3. Allows for shifts of focus and access to new perspectives on your experience.
>
> 4. Allows a forum for more feelings to come up.

5. Provides a reality base that continually contradicts the lie that talking about the abuse will result in dire consequences.

Each time the story of abuse is told — whenever a survivor is listened to with caring and awareness — another piece of healing takes place. As the story is repeated, more details are recovered. Whole chunks of childhood which had been forgotten can be recovered. This is not always a pleasant experience, but it is immensely valuable.[7]

Friendships

The greatest gift exchanged between men in our men's groups is the creation of strong friendships. Men who befriend other men are helping to create a new generation of loyal, intimate, confident, and trustworthy men and fathers who will invigorate and renew father-son relationships.

Stuart Miller in *Men and Friendship* offers some wonderful ideas for men and their quest for healthy male friendships. "Bold acts of consciousness are, I think, the true basis for an art of friendship these days. No gimmicks will work. The arts of friendship we need are inner acts, acts of depth of the heart, of self-searching, and of decision."[8]

Miller goes on to say that male friendships can be thought of as a place in a man's inner being, a space in his life, that is occupied daily by another man, a place that is regularly charged with love, concern, thoughtfulness, and, sometimes, resentment, anger, even deep hurt. Engagement means emotional involvement.

True friendship implies commitment and the understanding that a friend will be there and will not let go. It implies that a friend will maintain the engagement in the face of obstacles, misunderstandings, and temptations, and that a friend is prepared to undertake inconveniences, even sacrifices.

True male friendship is personal. The relationship is its own context. Friendship may arise from another relationship —

for example, work — but it is not dependent upon it. Male friendship is just one man with another.[9]

Martin W. Pable talks about a man's quest for love. He reminds us that "it is no secret that the need for love is probably the strongest drive within our personality." Back in the 1930s the brilliant psychoanalyst Karen Horney hypothesized that every newborn infant experiences what she called "basic anxiety." She described it as "the feeling of being alone and helpless in a potentially hostile world." To counteract basic anxiety, the infant needs the warm, caring presence of other human persons. Children who grow up without stable, loving people around them will be vulnerable to anxiety all their lives, Horney believed. Furthermore, all human beings have this built-in desire for relationship with others. In any case, our experiences of loneliness are powerful testimonies to "the quest for love."[10]

Men will satisfy their quest for love only when they maintain healthy, interdependent relationships with other men. The need for masculine human love and its potency and virile expression can be satisfied only by another man.

> If I am to love other men as I love myself, I shall have to show them many of the same things I want to show women. My analysis of love of the self, both embodied and spiritual, suggests that a tender care is often the prime desideratum. There is no reason that should not be true for men's love of one another. Just as one can rightly add that love of self also has to include discipline and challenge, one can rightly add that good male friends keep one another on their toes. But at the core of the male friendships I most treasure, as at the core of the love I received from my father . . . is an acceptance both gentle and unconditional. My father did not push me faster than I wanted to go, perhaps because he observed that I was already pushing myself. . . . My best friends do tell me the truth. They speak up when they think I am wrong. But the wider context always makes it clear that whether or not I accept what they have to say, they will continue to love me.[11]

Chapter 14

Masculinity Revisited

For us to explore any new patterns of fathering and father styles, we need to seriously consider the blueprints of manhood that will guide us along the way. Our understanding of manhood either limits and hinders our fathering capacities or provides us with newfound energies that catapult us into new dimensions of fatherhood.

A Masculine Body

The male body is a primary arena where men explore how special and unique they are. Male biology determines how men demonstrate their manhood and deliver their fathering skills. This fact cannot be underestimated.

Anthropologist David Gilmore has found that men the world over have generic criteria of manhood and male roles. A definition of a man in any culture includes competency in three areas.

The first is *provisioning*. A real man provides for his wife, his children, and his group — whether he's a Turk fisherman or a Masai cattleman. He has to create a surplus. This is still "the big one" in Western society as well; the breadwinner, until the last couple of decades, was almost always a male.

The second is *protecting*. Defending your clan, your country, is almost exclusively a male duty. No nation in the world drafts women for combat. You don't send women of childbearing age to their deaths if you want your society to survive.

The third is *impregnating*. In many cultures, having lots of children and wives or mistresses shows that you're a real man.

Many cultures regard true manhood as "a prize to be won or wrested through struggle." Societies are fragile; they can die away and disintegrate or be taken over by their neighbors. To make the transition from boyhood to manhood, a male must display traits and skills the society needs to survive. Historically, those male roles have involved risk-taking, aggressiveness, defense, strength, stoicism, competence, competitiveness, and sexual proficiency. That's where the tests of manhood and the male rites of passage come in. For instance, men are not necessarily warlike — although there's a little bit of the warrior in us because of our testosterone; rather bellicosity has to be encouraged, shaped by the culture. And cultures do this because in many cases machismo has helped them survive.

There may not be a universal male or female, but there's no way to discount millions of years of evolution, according to Gilmore. Male and female sex hormones are very different, and they influence us to behave in distinct ways. Culture then takes those biological givens and exaggerates or suppresses them. Some cultures have come close to extinguishing the biological differences between men and women.[1]

Melvin Konner notes that males of all ages in virtually every culture are more physically aggressive than females. Males also surpass females in risk-taking and thrill-seeking.

Natural selection prepared men to be hunters, and we've departed from that role only in the past 10,000 years, a short time in evolutionary terms. We [men] are, in effect, hunters in business suits. Perhaps that's one reason why, in the United States alone, more than 400 people are slain each week, most of them by men. Feminists may joke about "testosterone poisoning," but the fact is that this male hormone does play a strong role in aggression.

Indeed, convicts serving time for violent crimes tend to have higher testosterone levels than nonviolent inmates, according to studies at Georgia State University.[2]

A man's body and his particular masculine energy must be understood from a man's point of view. Men learn to manage their bodies and their formed body image from what they have observed in their fathers. From their fathers, men learn how to contain their physical and emotional strength and how to place themselves in relationship to others. Each father, knowingly or unknowingly, provides his son with a "container" to carry his strength, power, and stamina into life. A son without a workable container is unable to access his healthy and natural desires for masculine expression. A son does not receive his container from his mother. A mother teaches her son how to access the fluids of life (emotions). The son also learns from his mother how to embody his own affectivity, which can be achieved only if his container is intact. A son's ability to carry his emotions, the fluids held in the container, can be accessed and managed well only if his father helped his son to build a strong and healthy container.

Robert Bly recounts a story that demonstrates the son's need for a container from his father.

One woman...was raising a son and two daughters. When the son was fourteen or so he went off to live with his father, but stayed only a month or two and then came back. She said she knew that, with three women, there was too much feminine energy in the house for him. It was unbalanced, so to speak, but what could she do?

One day something strange happened. She said gently, "John, it's time to come to dinner," and he knocked her across the room. She said, "I think it's time to go back to your father." He said, "You're right." The boy couldn't bring what he needed into consciousness, but his *body* knew it. And his body acted. The mother didn't take it personally, either. She understood it was a message. In the United States there are so many big-muscled high school boys hulking around the kitchen rudely, and I think in a way they're trying to make themselves less attractive to their mothers. Separation from the mother is crucial. I'm not saying that women have been doing the wrong thing necessarily. I think the problem is more that the men are not really doing their job.[3]

A man learns from his father and other men how to manage his container and how to reflect to the world his body image. A man's body image is his first demonstration to the world community and to other men and women who he is as man, father, male. A man's body image reflects his inner content. It helps him to communicate his particular and unique masculine energy and to feel, embrace, express, contain, and control his thoughts, feelings, and behavior. A son learns how a man's biology is to be integrated and cared for from his father and from other male role models.

A young boy of a single parent yelled at his mother, who had just corrected him about how messy his clothes had gotten while playing with his friends. Terry, the young boy, had never seen his biological father. When Terry came running into the kitchen for a glass of water, the conversation between him and his mother went like this:

MOM: Terry, your clothes are just a dirty mess!

TERRY: Well, Mom, that's what boys do when they play.

MOM: But can't you play and not get so dirty and ruin your clothes?

TERRY: Mom, stop asking me to play like a girl!

MOM: It's just that you are so hard on your clothes and shoes. You'll have to change your clothes and I'll put them in the wash.

TERRY: Being dirty is a boy's world. Stop trying to wash *it* out of me. I don't want to be like you and the other girls. Leave us boys alone so we can be who we really are.

Terry then ran off with his friends who were waiting for his escape. He and his friends were soon back on the dirt pile. Terry exemplified a boy's need to be a boy with his own body image.

> The newly emerging image of sacred masculinity is a creative, fecund, generative, nurturing, protective, and compassionate male, existing in harmony with the earth and the feminine, yet also erotic, free, wild, playful, energetic, and fierce. This image is a far cry from the invincible, rigid, patriarchal, war-making hero, the silently suffering martyr, or the feminized "soft" male who serves the goddess.[4]

A Masculine Spirit

Spirituality is integral to our world. Men and women of prayer reflect well their values and beliefs. Unfortunately, much of spirituality today does not relate well or honestly with the male spirit that longs for embodiment with healthy masculinity. Men who want to recover their authentic selves need to be mentored by other men who have already achieved some familiarity with their manhood through prayer and other spiritual disciplines. Much of what men try to experience in the area of prayer and spirituality has left them emasculated. Healthy male spirituality embraces a man's raw masculinity and affirms its goodness. It gives permission for expression that may be viewed as crude, lacking grace and elegance, and physical in its impact and expression. When a man prays, his very nature demands engagement with his sexual self and body image.

A man who engages God with his body image will have a sexual stance in his spirituality that is procreative, re-creative, and transformative. A man's spirituality is procreative insofar as it is involved in producing, building, creating, erecting, designing, birthing, and sustaining life.

A man's spirituality will not be complete unless there lies within and without a re-creative attitude that seeks a quest. The adventures of a man's spirituality must involve risk, daring, threat, challenge, struggle, conquest, competition, and involvement that physically engages his body. If a man is reduced to the role of passive observer, he will not be able to tap the wealth of creative powers lying within him.

When a man prays from his male nature and uses his healthy masculinity to touch the spirit of God, he will know joy. A man participates in the transformation of prayer not just as a provider or participant, but as a generous distributor of what he has received. A man's nature, when lived through a healthy masculinity, is apostolic in expression. The transformation experienced by men of prayer can give rise to a new generation of wise men who know the way to holiness.

A man's spirituality is by nature social. In *A Man and His God*, Martin W. Pable has noted that there are a lot of males in our society who are not satisfied with pursuing the Great American Dream of wealth, status, success, and power. They either know intuitively or have learned by experience that the dream is more illusion than reality, at least in its capacity to provide genuine happiness and fulfillment. So these men are looking for something deeper, something they may not always name. But they know it has more to do with inner reality than with outward appearance, something more spiritual than material.[5]

A man with strong spiritual values welcomes these as an integral part of himself. He finds it almost impossible to separate his spiritual life from his work place. John Carmody says,

> If I were more clearly involved in a romance with the Holy Spirit than has been the leitmotif of my spiritual life to date, I also might do a better job at overcoming the dualism that seems to afflict all human beings, but perhaps especially men. This dualism appears in the masculine struggle to keep sexual appetite and love together and maintain an integral image of women.[6]

Most men in their search for spiritual fulfillment and maturity are confused in their understanding of "ecstasy." Many men have a brief introduction to ecstasy when they experience their first intimate relationship. The powerful fusion of loving, lusting, and longing are momentarily fulfilled. Unfortunately, it is only momentary. The only way to maintain the brief satisfaction of love-ecstasy is to keep depending on human encounters and relationships.

There are also unnatural ways to achieve ecstasy. Robert Johnson dedicated one of his books to the understanding of the psychology of joy that he calls ecstasy. He reminds us that all addictions are the negative side of spiritual seeking. We are looking for an exultation of the spirit, but instead of fulfillment we get a short-lived physical thrill that can never satisfy the chronic, gnawing emptiness with which we are beset. To fill this emptiness, we need to reconnect with the capacity for ecstasy that lies dormant within us. Our first step must be to try to understand the nature of ecstasy.[7]

Some people look for ecstasy in all the wrong places.

> Craving spiritual ecstasy, we mistakenly seek material fulfillment. We chase after a phantom, and when we catch it — in the form of more money, more food, more sex, more drugs, more drinks, more oblivion — we find that we have been chasing ephemeral happiness when we should have invited lasting joy. What do we do next? We will use intellectual power at our command to fill the void. We read books and take classes, looking for "the answer."[8]

But the answer can be found only when a man looks within himself and comes to know himself as one created in God's image and likeness.

Some of the ecstatic relationships a man encounters will provide a prelude to the real thing. A man's quest for ecstasy — that emotional encounter too powerful for a man's body to contain or his rational mind to understand and that transports him to another realm — can be achieved only under the following conditions:

1. A man has a masculine container to begin his quest for ecstasy.

2. He is mentored by another man in the ways of masculine spirituality and is companioned along the way.

3. He does not rely upon a woman or woman's love to help him to attain ecstasy.

4. He separates *happiness*, which is short-lived, from *joy*, which is an exultation of the spirit, a gladness or delight with the beatitude of heaven or paradise.

5. He begins his journey inward in order to become at home with the irrational and unexplored areas of his inner life. Then he expresses to the outer world new gestures, rituals, and body expressions.

Eventually, a man will discover the awareness that God was always present, asleep within himself. He will discover a living God who loves him as man.

A Masculine Heart

"Inferiority feelings, the power drive, anxiety, possessiveness, envy, jealousy, and the compulsion to subdue and conquer are the mainsprings of the patriarchal ego," according to Edward C. Whitmont. A similar assessment is given by Jean Bolen in *Gods in Everyman:*

> Patriarchal values that emphasize the acquisition of power, rational thinking, and being in control are unconsciously or consciously enforced by mothers and fathers, peers, schools, and other institutions that reward and punish boys and men for their behavior. As a result, men must learn to conform and to stifle their individuality along with their emotions.[9]

Men need to explore their inner blueprints, which distinguish them in their expressions, feelings, and emotions. Vulnerability, feeling, intellect, strength and courage do not belong exclusively to either men or women. These qualities are the common heritage of humanity. Emotion is part of all human beings.

As Maurice Champagne-Gilbert states,

Men should be less concerned with conquering space or inventing major new technologies; their real challenge lies in conquering a new relationship with life, a relationship in which the values traditionally labeled as feminine are repossessed by men as existential values.[10]

A masculine heart has its own pathways to excellence. Each man needs to have the opportunity to awaken within himself the beauty, order, and truth of his masculine nature. In doing so, his heart will be awakened, empowering him to become a father worthy of honor.

Conclusion

To Be a Man, To Be a Father

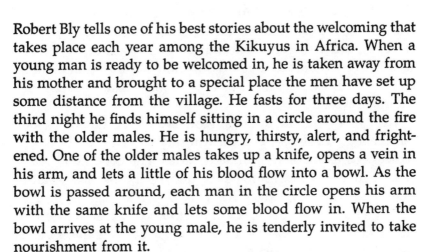

Robert Bly tells one of his best stories about the welcoming that takes place each year among the Kikuyus in Africa. When a young man is ready to be welcomed in, he is taken away from his mother and brought to a special place the men have set up some distance from the village. He fasts for three days. The third night he finds himself sitting in a circle around the fire with the older males. He is hungry, thirsty, alert, and frightened. One of the older males takes up a knife, opens a vein in his arm, and lets a little of his blood flow into a bowl. As the bowl is passed around, each man in the circle opens his arm with the same knife and lets some blood flow in. When the bowl arrives at the young male, he is tenderly invited to take nourishment from it.

The boy learns that there is a kind of nourishment that comes not from his mother, but from males. And he learns that the knife can be used for purposes besides wounding others. Can he have any doubts now that he is welcome in the male world? Once this ritual is carried out, the older males can teach him the myths, the stories, the songs that embody male values, not fighting only, but spirit values.[1]

When a culture ceases to provide specific, meaningful initiatory pathways, the individual male psyche is left to initiate itself. And therein lies a great danger, visible in the kinds of initiation to which many men turn:

street gangs, drug and alcohol abuse, high-risk sports, militarism, discipleship to charismatic cult leaders, obsessive work place competition, compulsive relocation of home and job, serial sexual conquests, pursuit of the "perfect" (and thus unattainable) older male mentor, and so forth.[2]

Today more than ever in the history of our world community, we are in need of men who will mentor other men into manhood and fatherhood. We need healthy men who will provide us with opportunities to practice and to experiment with our manhood. We need men who will care for us and our masculinity, men who will not shy away from the added responsibilities of confrontation, men who will challenge us to live up to our potential. We need men who will sacrifice themselves in order to usher into our broken world other men of well-being who are at home with their natural gifts of masculinity. We need older males to welcome younger males into the male world.

We live by our definitions. How we define ourselves, our fatherhood, manhood, and masculinity directly limits or enhances our expression of these realities. The good news today is that men are redefining their understanding of a healthy male. Men are no longer limited to perceiving themselves through the lived experiences of their father or their father's father. They have within their reach a new attitude that enables them to glean from past generations what is healthy and lifegiving. Men are opening themselves up to a more profound understanding of themselves as men who will father the next generation.

Many men I have worked with around the country have shared with me and with others what they have found helpful for their recovery process, how they have reclaimed their fatherhood and fulfilled their unmet father needs. The wisdom of these men testifies to the great potential that lies within each man who is willing to look within himself and to begin the healing process. The collective knowledge and wisdom shared by these men may help you to claim your rights and privileges as a healthy man who can parent and nurture — one who can be fathered and who can father in turn.

TO ANY LITTLE BOY'S FATHER

There are little eyes upon you
And they're watching night and day;
There are little ears that quickly
Take in everything you say.

There are little hands all eager
To do everything you do;
And a little boy who's dreaming
Of the day he'll be like you.

You're the little fellow's idol;
You're the wisest of the wise.
In his little mind, about you
No suspicions ever rise.

He believes in you devoutly,
Holds that all you say and do,
He will say and do in your way,
When he's grown up, just like you.

There's a wide-eyed little fellow
Who believes you're always right;
And his ears are always open
And he watches day and night.

You are setting an example
Every day in all you do;
For the little boy who's watching
To grow up and be like you.

— Anonymous
Emmaus Centre, Trinidad, 1993

Epilogue

The Male's Journey:
Men Mentoring Men

The following story has been used at various men's conferences to help participants remember those significant men who have helped them imagine their masculine potential in their own lives. After the story has been read aloud or privately, list those men who have stood behind you and helped you to imagine your masculine potential. If you find yourself unable to remember any such affirming males in your life, choose some men whom you admire and imagine them standing behind you. Who could you become if you had these men as your models, mentors, and advocates? Describe your masculine potential as you borrow attributes and attitudes from those males who could usher you in to becoming a healthy man, friend, husband, father.

This is a story about a young boy and how he becomes a strong man.

There is a lake outside the village that is powerful. It is a mystical and holy place. No one can go to the lake alone and benefit from its life-transforming powers. One has to be met by a guide, one who has been to the lake before and experienced the transformation himself.

A boy knows from within himself when the time has arrived

for him to visit the lake. It is unfailing knowledge, intuitive, imprinted in his very being.

He may look as though he is wandering aimlessly as he approaches the lake, but sooner or later he will discover the particular place where he is to begin his rite of passage. A boy will spend days and nights at the lake, waiting for the transformation from boyhood to manhood, for that is his purpose there. He will take time to play, exploring the edge of the lake, and he will walk around the entire lake to enjoy all its abundant life. Swimming and bathing, floating and playing in the waters are necessary rituals. He must learn to feed himself with the food provided by the lake; he must comb both land and sea for the many treasures to be found along the beaches and in the lake's deep waters. In so doing, he develops a sense of wonder and awe — prerequisites for his imminent transformation.

Through the day, the lake takes on various expressions and characteristics. Sometimes the waters are dark and murky, sometimes calm and peaceful. Sometimes the lake makes waves and splashes, laughingly, along its shores. Sometimes its waves seem vicious and heartless, powerful and destructive. And sometimes, in the early hours of the morning, the waters of the lake offer a quiet stillness, deep and rich.

It is only in those moments — when the waters are as still as glass — that the boy can be delivered into manhood. For as he looks into the still waters of the lake, he can see an image of himself. Gazing into the stillness, he can begin to imagine his gifts and talents; his future can be dreamed. He is, however, only a boy, and he can see only a boy's image, and no more. He cannot yet see a man.

The boy's longing for something more than himself and his own image grows stronger. What he sees of himself in the lake is only a small suggestion of what he might be. It is the image of a real man that is the catalyst he needs. If he is to be a man, he must be able to see a man: no boy can become a man by himself.

If the boy waits at the lake too long and does not receive the help of another significant male, he may lose heart and fall prey to impatience or despair, vulnerable to the dangers that must be reckoned with if he is to succeed. If he spends too much time playing and not learning to discipline himself, resting too little, he will not have the energy to awaken during the early morning hours and catch the still waters of the lake. If a girl or boy his age stands behind him and looks into the water with him, he may be distracted from his goal: he will see only another child's image — one not much different from his own and therefore unable to draw him into maturity. If it is a mature woman whose reflection meets his own and he tries to force the rite of passage by using her as his guiding image, he will lose access to his male energy and power. He will instead become absorbed by his own feminine powers and begin his movement into adulthood with confusion and inhospitality toward his own masculinity and male expressions of manhood, brotherhood, and fatherhood.

The happy ending of this story occurs when the boy looks into the still waters of the lake and sees an older significant male standing behind him. *The image of the man enraptures and surrounds the image of the boy, and the boy becomes a man.* The naive child can identify and recognize a new potential; integrating it, he can claim for himself a mature, confident, and stable masculine identity. Affirmed in his masculinity, he is able now to embody a man's way of living. He can envision his power, authority, emotions, and relationships — not through his child's eyes any longer, but through the eyes of a man. The new image available to him enables him to expand, to grow and develop his masculine identity. Inner strength, serenity, courage, and adventure are but a few of the gifts bestowed on the boy who completes his rite of passage.

And bearing the precious gift of manhood itself, he is empowered for yet another vital task and privilege: he, too, can revisit the lake to be the significant male for another boy — fathering the next generation.

Notes

Introduction: Fathers and Sons

1. Samuel Osherson, *Finding Our Fathers: How a Man's Life Is Shaped by His Relationship with His Father* (New York: Fawcett Columbine, 1986), 6.

2. Lewis Yablonsky, *Fathers and Sons* (New York: Simon & Schuster, 1982), 32.

3. Ibid., 48.

4. Ibid., 13.

5. See James Henderson, "The Role of the Father in Separation-Individuation," *Bulletin of the Menninger Clinic* 16, no. 3 (May 1982): 231–54.

6. Osherson, *Finding Our Fathers.*

7. Kyle D. Pruett, M.D., *The Nurturing Father: Journey Toward the Complete Man* (New York: Warner Books, 1987).

8. Michael E. Lamb, *The Role of the Father in Child Development* (New York: Wiley-Interscience, 1976), 15.

9. Ibid., 18–20.

10. Ibid., 22–23.

11. Robert Moore and Douglas Gillette, *King, Warrior, Magician, Lover: Rediscovering the Archetypes of the Mature Masculine.* San Francisco: HarperSanFrancisco, 1990), xv.

12. Osherson, *Finding Our Fathers*, 6.

13. Leonard P. LeSourd, *Strong Men Weak Men: Godly Strength and the Male Identity* (Old Tappan, N.J.: Chosen Books, 1990), 114.

14. P. Nicolson, "A Brief Report of Women's Expectations of Men's Behavior in the Transition to Parenthood: Contradictions and Conflicts for Counseling Psychology Practice," *Counselling Psychology Quarterly* 3, no. 1 (1990): 353–61.

15. Pruett, *The Nurturing Father*, 39.

16. Kyle D. Pruett, M.D., *The Underground Father* (New York: Warner Books, 1987), 39–40.

17. John R. Moreland, "Nuclear Family Break-up as an Impetus for Male Change," paper presented at the annual convention of the American Psychological Association, Anaheim, Calif., August 26–30, 1983.

Chapter 4: The Magician Father

1. Robert Moore and Douglas Gillette, *King, Warrior, Magician, Lover: Rediscovering the Archetypes of the Mature Masculine*. San Francisco: HarperSanFrancisco, 1990), 114–15.
2. Ibid., 115.

Chapter 11: Inner Work

1. Robert Moore and Douglas Gillette, *King, Warrior, Magician, Lover: Rediscovering the Archetypes of the Mature Masculine*. San Francisco: HarperSanFrancisco, 1990), xix.
2. Ibid., 7.
3. Guy Corneau, *Absent Fathers, Lost Sons: The Search for Masculine Identity* (Boston: Shambhala, 1991), 181.
4. Ibid., 176.
5. David Keirsey and Marilyn Bates provide an excellent survey of character and temperament types in their book *Please Understand Me: Character and Temperament Types* (Del Mar, Calif.: Prometheus Book Company, 1984).
6. Maria Beesing, O.P., Robert J. Nogosek, C.S.C., and Patrick H. O'Leary, S.J., *The Enneagram: A Journey of Self Discovery* (Denville, N.J.: Dimension Books, 1984), 6.
7. Ibid., 3.

Chapter 12: Second-Chance Fathers

1. Patricia Berry, ed., *Fathers and Mothers*, 2d ed. (Dallas: Spring Publications, 1990), 2–3.
2. Guy Corneau, *Absent Fathers, Lost Sons: The Search for Masculine Identity* (Boston: Shambhala, 1991), 175–76.
3. John Friel, *The Grown-up Man: Hope, Hurt, Healing, Heroes, and Honor* (Deerfield Beach, Fla.: Health Communications, 1991), 78.
4. Mary Ann Lamanna and Agnes Reidmann, *Marriages and Family: Making Choices and Facing Change*, 3d ed. (Belmont, Calif.: Wadsworth Publishing Company, 1981), 284.

Chapter 13: Men Fathering Men

1. Guy Corneau, *Absent Fathers, Lost Sons: The Search for Masculine Identity* (Boston: Shambhala, 1991), 178–79.

2. Robert Moore and Douglas Gillette, *King, Warrior, Magician, Lover: Rediscovering the Archetypes of the Mature Masculine.* San Francisco: HarperSanFrancisco, 1990), 6–7.

3. Louis W. McLeod and Bruce K. Pemberton, "Men Together in Group Therapy," in Keith Thompson, ed., *To Be a Man: In Search of the Deep Masculine* (Los Angeles: Jeremy P. Tarcher, 1991), 239.

4. Ibid., 242–43.

5. The most useful book I can recommend on the subject of male sexual abuse is Mike Lew, *Victims No Longer: Men Recovering from Incest and Other Sexual Child Abuse* (New York: Nevraumont, 1988).

6. Ibid., 63.

7. Ibid., 198–200.

8. Stuart Miller, *Men and Friendship* (Bath, Eng.: Gateway Books, 1983), 195.

9. Ibid., 191.

10. Martin W. Pable, O.F.M. Cap., *Contemporary Male Spirituality: A Man and His God* (Notre Dame, Ind.: Ave Maria Press, 1988), 73–74.

11. John Carmody, *Toward a Male Spirituality* (Mystic, Conn.: Twenty-Third Publications, 1987), 55–56.

Chapter 14: Masculinity Revisited

1. Michael Lafavore, *Men's Health Advisor 1992* (Emmaus, Pa.: Rodale Press, 1992), 89–91.

2. Cited in ibid., 80.

3. In Keith Thompson, ed., *To Be a Man: In Search of the Deep Masculine* (Los Angeles: Jeremy P. Tarcher, 1991), 41–42.

4. Ibid., 25.

5. Martin W. Pable, O.F.M. Cap., *Contemporary Male Spirituality: A Man and His God* (Notre Dame, Ind.: Ave Maria Press, 1988), 121.

6. John Carmody, *Toward a Male Spirituality* (Mystic, Conn.: Twenty-Third Publications, 1987), 35.

7. Robert A. Johnson, *Ecstasy: Understanding the Psychology of Joy* (San Francisco: Harper & Row, 1987), vii.

8. Ibid., 20.

9. Jean S. Bolen, *Gods in Every Man: A New Psychology of Men's Lives and Loves* (New York: Harper & Row, 1989), 13.

10. Cited in Guy Corneau, *Absent Fathers, Lost Sons: The Search for Masculine Identity* (Boston: Shambhala, 1991), 175.

Conclusion: To Be a Man, To Be a Father

1. Robert Bly in Keith Thompson, ed., *To Be a Man: In Search of the Deep Masculine* (Los Angeles: Jeremy P. Tarcher, 1991) 39.

2. Ibid., 37.

Suggested Readings

Men

Absher, T. *Men and the Goddess: Feminine Archetypes in Western Literature.* Rochester, Vt.: Park Street Press, 1990.

Barnhouse, R. T., and U. T. Holmes III. *Male & Female: Christian Approaches to Sexuality.* New York: Seabury Press, 1976.

Bausch, W. J. *Becoming a Man.* Mystic, Conn.: Twenty-Third Publications, 1988.

Becker, V. *The Real Man Inside.* Grand Rapids: Zondervan Publishing House, 1992.

Berry, P., ed. *Fathers and Mothers.* 2d ed. Dallas: Spring Publications, 1990.

Bly, R. *Iron John: A Book about Men.* Reading, Mass.: Addison-Wesley, 1990.

Bolen, J. S. *Gods in Every Man: A New Psychology of Men's Lives and Loves.* New York: Harper & Row, 1989.

Carmody, J. *Toward a Male Spirituality.* Mystic, Conn.: Twenty-Third Publications, 1987.

Corneau, G. *Absent Fathers, Lost Sons: The Search for Masculine Identity.* Boston: Shambhala, 1991.

Edinger, E. F. *The Creation of Consciousness: Jung's Myth for Modern Man.* Toronto: Inner City Books, 1984.

Elium, D., and J. Elium. *Raising a Son: Parents and the Making of a Healthy Man.* Hillsboro, Ore.: Beyond Words Publishing, 1992.

Estrada, H. *Recovery for Male Victims of Child Abuse.* Santa Fe, N.M.: Red Rabbit Press, 1990.

Firestone, R., ed. *The Man in Me.* New York: Harper Collins, 1978.

Friel, J. *The Grown-up Man: Hope, Hurt, Healing, Heroes, and Honor.* Deerfield Beach, Fla.: Health Communications, 1991.

Guzie, T., and N. Guzie. *About Men and Women: How Your "Great Story" Shapes Your Destiny.* Mahwah, N.J.: Paulist Press, 1986.

Harding, C., ed. *Wingspan: Inside the Men's Movement.* New York: St. Martin's Press, 1992.

Hopcke, R. H. *Men's Dreams, Men's Healing.* Boston: Shambhala, 1990.

187

Iatestra, R. R. *Fathers: A Fresh Start for the Christian Family*. Ann Arbor: Servant Publications, 1980.

Jackson, G. *The Secret Lore of Gardening*. Toronto: Inner City Books, 1991.

Johnson, R. A. *He: Understanding Masculine Psychology*. New York: Harper & Row, 1977.

———. *Transformation: Understanding the Three Levels of Masculine Consciousness*. San Francisco: Harper Collins, 1991.

Jung, C. G. *Man and His Symbols*. New York: Dell, 1964.

Keen, S. *Fire in the Belly: On Being a Man*. New York: Bantam Books, 1991.

———. *Inward Bound: Exploring the Geography of Your Emotions*. New York: Bantam Books, 1992.

Keirsey, D., and M. Bates. *Please Understand Me: Character and Temperament Types*. Del Mar, Calif.: Prometheus, 1984.

Kipnis, A. R. *Knights without Armor: Practical Guide for Men in Quest of Masculine Soul*. Los Angeles: Jeremy P. Tarcher, 1991.

Lamanna, M., and A. Reidmann. *Marriage and Families Making Choices and Facing Change*. 3d ed. Belmont, Calif.: Wadsworth Publishing Company, 1981.

Lafavore, M. *Men's Health Advisor 1992*. Emmaus, Pa.: Rodale Press, 1992.

Lee, J. *The Flying Boy: Healing the Wounded Man*. Deerfield Beach, Fla.: Health Communications, 1987.

———. *At My Father's Wedding: Reclaiming Our True Masculinity*. New York: Bantam Books, 1991.

LeSourd, L. E. *Strong Men Weak Men: Godly Strength and the Male Identity*. Old Tappan, N.J.: Chosen Books, 1990.

Lew, M. *Victims No Longer: Men Recovering from Incest and Other Sexual Child Abuse*. New York: Nevraumont, 1988.

McAllaster, E. *When a Father Is Hard to Honor*. Elgin, Ill.: Brethren Press, 1984.

McGill, M. E. *The McGill Report on Male Intimacy*. New York: Harper & Row, 1985.

McNeely, D. A. *Animus Aeternus: Exploring the Inner Masculine*. Toronto: Inner City Books, 1991.

Miller, S. *Men and Friendship*. Bath, England: Gateway Books, 1983.

Monick, E. *Phallos, Sacred Image of the Masculine*. Toronto: Inner City Books, 1987.

———. *Castration and Male Rage: The Phallic Wound*. Toronto: Inner City Books, 1991.

Moore, Robert, and Douglas Gillette. *King, Warrior, Magician, Lover: Rediscovering the Archetypes of the Mature Masculine*. San Francisco: HarperSanFrancisco, 1990.

———. *The King Within: Assessing the King in the Male Psyche*. New York: William Morrow & Co., 1992.

Neill, M., R. Chervin, and D. Briel. *How Shall We Find the Father?* New York: Seabury Press, 1983.

Nerburn, K. *Letters to My Son: Reflections on Becoming a Man*. San Rafael, Calif.: New World Library, 1993.

Osherson, S. *Finding Our Fathers: How a Man's Life Is Shaped by His Relationship with His Father.* New York: Fawcett Columbine, 1986.

Ornstein, Y. *From the Hearts of Men.* New York: Fawcett Columbine, 1991.

Pable, M. W. *Contemporary Male Spirituality: A Man and His God.* Notre Dame, Ind.: Ave Maria Press, 1988.

Pearson, C. *The Hero Within.* San Francisco: Harper & Row, 1986.

Pederson, L. E. *Dark Hearts: The Unconscious Forces That Shape Men's Lives.* Boston: Shambhala, 1991.

Pruett, K. D. *The Nurturing Father: Journey toward the Complete Man.* New York: Warner Books, 1987.

Pyle, H. *The Garden behind the Moon.* New York: Parabola Books, 1988.

Robinson, B. E., and R. L. Barrett. *The Developing Father: Emerging Roles in Contemporary Society.* New York: Guilford Press, 1986.

Rohr, R., and J. Martos. *The Wild Man's Journey: Reflections on Male Spirituality.* Cincinnati: St. Anthony Messenger Press, 1992.

Samuels, A. *The Father: Contemporary Jungian Perspectives.* New York: University Press, 1985.

Sanford, J. A. *The Invisible Partners.* New York: Paulist Press, 1980.

———. *The Man Who Lost His Shadow.* New York: Paulist Press, 1983.

Sanford, J. A., and G. Lough. *What Men Are Like.* New York: Paulist Press, 1988.

Scull, C., ed. *Fathers, Sons, and Daughters: Exploring Fatherhood, Renewing the Bond.* Los Angeles: Jeremy P. Tarcher, 1992.

Shapiro, J. L. *When Men Are Pregnant: Needs and Concerns of Expectant Fathers.* San Luis Obispo, Calif.: Impact Publications, 1987.

Stone, H., and S. Winkelman. *Embracing Each Other.* San Rafael, Calif.: New World Library, 1989.

Thompson, K., ed. *To Be a Man: In Search of the Deep Masculine.* Los Angeles: Jeremy P. Tarcher, 1991.

Vogt, G. M., and S. T. Sirridge. *Like Son, Like Father: Healing the Father-Son Wound in Men's Lives.* New York: Plenum Press, 1991.

Von Franz, M. L. *Puer Aeternus.* Boston: Sigo Press, 1981.

Weiner, B. *Boy into Man: A Father's Guide to Initiation of Teenage Sons.* San Francisco: Transformation Press, 1992.

Wyly, J. *The Phallic Quest: Priapus and Masculine Inflation.* Toronto: Inner City Books, 1989.

Yablonsky, L. *Fathers and Sons.* New York: Simon & Schuster, 1982.

Myers-Briggs Type Indicator (MBTI)

Faucett, R., and C. Faucett. *Personality and Spiritual Freedom: Personality Type and Myers-Briggs.* New York: Doubleday, 1987.

Jung, C. G. *Psychological Types.* Princeton, N.J.: Princeton University Press, 1976.

Keating, C. J. *Who We Are Is How We Pray: Matching Personality and Spirituality.* Mystic, Conn.: Twenty-Third Publications, 1987.

Keirsey, D., and M. Bates. *Please Understand Me: Character and Temperament Types.* Del Mar, Calif.: Prometheus, 1984.

Kroeger, O., and J. M. Thuesen. *Type Talk: Or How to Determine Your Personality Type and Change Your Life.* New York: Delacorte Press, 1988.

Mamchur, C. M. *Insights: Understanding Yourself and Others.* Canada: Ontario Institute for Studies in Education, 1984.

Michael, C. P., and M. C. Norrisey. *Prayer and Temperament: Different Prayer Forms for Different Personality Types.* Charlottesville, Va.: The Open Door, 1984.

Myers, I. B. *Introduction to Type.* Palo Alto, Calif.: Consulting Psychologists Press, 1989.

Myers, I. B., and P. Myers. *Gifts Differing: MBTI.* Palo Alto, Calif.: Consulting Psychologists Press, 1980.

O'Conner, P. *Understanding Jung, Understanding Yourself.* New York: Paulist Press, 1985.

Schemel, G. J., and J. A. Borbely. *Facing Your Type.* Wernersville, Pa.: Typrofile Press, 1982.

Sharp, D. *Personality Types: Jung's Model of Typology.* Toronto: Inner City Books, 1987.

Enneagram

Beesing, M., R. J. Nogosek, and P. H. O'Leary. *The Enneagram: A Journey of Self Discovery.* Denville, N.J.: Dimension Books, 1984.

Keyes, M. F. *Emotions and the Enneagram: Working Through Your Shadow Life Script.* Muir Beach, Calif.: Molysdatur Publications, 1990.

————. *The Enneagram Cats of Muir Beach.* Muir Beach, Calif.: Molysdatur Publications, 1990.

Metz, B., and J. Burchill. *The Enneagram and Prayer: Discovering Our True Selves before God.* Denville, N.J.: Dimension Books, 1987.

Naranjo, C. *Ennea-Type Structures: Self-Analysis for the Seeker.* Nevada City, Calif.: Gateways/IDHHB, 1990.

Palmer, H. *The Enneagram: Understanding Yourself and the Others in Your Life.* San Francisco: Harper & Row, 1988.

Riso, D. R. *Personality Types: Using the Enneagram for Self-Discovery.* Boston: Houghton Mifflin, 1987.

————. *Understanding the Enneagram: Practical Guide to Personality Types.* Boston: Houghton Mifflin, 1990.

Tickerhoof, B. *Conversion and the Enneagram.* Denville, N.J.: Dimension Books, 1991.

Dreams

Bolen, J. S. *Goddesses in Everywoman: A New Psychology of Women.* New York: Harper & Row, 1984.

Clift, J. D., and B. Wallace. *Symbols of Transformation in Dreams*. New York: Crossroad, 1985.

Delaney, G. V. *Living Your Dreams*. San Francisco: Harper & Row, 1979.

Ferber, R. *Solve Your Child's Sleep Problems*. New York: Simon & Schuster, 1985.

Guggenbuhl-Craig, A. *Power in the Helping Professions*. Dallas: Spring Publications, 1971.

Hannah, B. *Encounters with the Soul: Active Imagination as Developed by C. G. Jung*. Boston: Sigo, 1981

Hartmann, E. *The Nightmare: The Psychology and Biology of Terrifying Dreams*. New York: Basic Books, 1984.

Hopcke, R. H. *Men's Dreams, Men's Healing*. Boston: Shambhala, 1990.

Johnson, R. A. *He: Understanding Masculine Psychology*. New York: Harper & Row, 1977.

———. *She: Understanding Feminine Psychology*. New York: Harper & Row, 1977.

———. *Inner Work*. San Francisco: Harper & Row, 1986.

———. *Ecstasy: Understanding the Psychology of Joy*. San Francisco: Harper & Row, 1987.

———. *Femininity Lost and Regained*. New York: HarperCollins, 1990.

Jung, C. G. *The Basic Writings of C. G. Jung*. New York: Random House, 1959.

———. *Man and His Symbols*. New York: Doubleday & Company, 1964.

———. *Memories, Dreams and Reflections*. New York: Random House, 1965.

Kellogg, J. *Mandala: Path of Beauty*. Williamsburg, Va.: Joan Kellogg, 1978.

Kelsey, M. T. *God, Dreams, and Revelation: A Christian Interpretation of Dreams*. Minneapolis: Augsburg Publishing House, 1974.

———. *Dreams: A Way to Listen to God*. New York: Paulist Press, 1978.

Miller, W. A. *Make Friends with Your Shadow: How to Accept and Use Positively the Negative Side of Your Personality*. Minneapolis: Augsburg Publishing House, 1982.

Reid, C. H. *Dreams: Discovering Your Inner Teacher*. Minneapolis: Winston Press, 1983.

Sanford, J. A. *Dreams, God's Forgotten Language*. New York: J. B. Lippincott, 1968.

———. *The Kingdom Within*. New York: Paulist Press, 1970.

———. *Healing and Wholeness*. New York: Paulist Press, 1977.

———. *Dreams and Healing: A Succinct and Lively Interpretation of Dreams*. New York: Paulist Press, 1978.

———. *The Invisible Partners*. New York: Paulist Press, 1980.

Savary, L. M., P. H. Berne, and S. K. Williams. *Dreams and Spiritual Growth: A Judeo-Christian Way of Dreamwork*. New York: Paulist Press, 1984.

Shulman, S., and J. Spencer. *Nightmare: The World of Terrifying Dreams*. New York: Macmillan, 1979.